The Arab Spring and the Geopolitics of the Middle East

Other Palgrave Pivot titles

Sandra L. Enos: **Service-Learning and Social Entrepreneurship in Higher Education: A Pedagogy of Social Change**

Fiona M. Hollands and Devayani Tirthali: **MOOCs in Higher Education: Institutional Goals and Paths Forward**

Geeta Nair: **Gendered Impact of Globalization of Higher Education: Promoting Human Development in India**

Geoffrey Till (editor): **The Changing Maritime Scene in Asia: Rising Tensions and Future Strategic Stability**

Simon Massey and Rino Coluccello (editors): **Eurafrican Migration: Legal, Economic and Social Responses to Irregular Migration**

Duncan McDuie-Ra: **Debating Race in Contemporary India**

Andrea Greenbaum: **The Tropes of War: Visual Hyperbole and Spectacular Culture**

Kristoffer Kropp: **A Historical Account of Danish Sociology: A Troubled Sociology**

Monika E. Reuter: **Creativity – A Sociological Approach**

M. Saiful Islam: **Pursuing Alternative Development: Indigenous People, Ethnic Organization and Agency**

Justin DePlato: **American Presidential Power and the War on Terror: Does the Constitution Matter?**

Christopher Perkins: **The United Red Army on Screen: Cinema, Aesthetics and The Politics of Memory**

Susanne Lundin: Organs for Sale: **An Ethnographic Examination of the International Organ Trade**

Margot Finn and Kate Smith (editors): **New Paths to Public Histories**

Gordon Ade-Ojo and Vicky Duckworth: **Adult Literacy Policy and Practice: From Intrinsic Values to Instrumentalism**

Brendan Howe (editors): **Democratic Governance in Northeast Asia: A Human-Centred Approach to Evaluating Democracy**

Evie Kendal: **Equal Opportunity and the Case for State Sponsored Ectogenesis**

Joseph Watras: **Philosophies of Environmental Education and Democracy: Harris, Dewey, and Bateson on Human Freedoms in Nature**

Christos Kourtelis: **The Political Economy of Euro-Mediterranean Relations: European Neighbourhood Policy in North Africa**

Liz Montegary and Melissa Autumn White (editors): **Mobile Desires: The Politics and Erotics of Mobility Justice**

palgrave▶**pivot**

The Arab Spring and the Geopolitics of the Middle East: Emerging Security Threats and Revolutionary Change

Amr Yossef
Independent Scholar

and

Joseph R. Cerami
Senior Lecturer, Bush School of Government, Texas, USA

palgrave
macmillan

DOI: 10.1057/9781137504081.0001

First published 2015 by
PALGRAVE MACMILLAN

Palgrave Macmillan in the UK is an imprint of Macmillan Publishers Limited, registered in England, company number 785998, of Houndmills, Basingstoke, Hampshire RG21 6XS.

Palgrave Macmillan in the US is a division of St Martin's Press LLC, 175 Fifth Avenue, New York, NY 10010.

Palgrave Macmillan is the global academic imprint of the above companies and has companies and representatives throughout the world.

Palgrave® and Macmillan® are registered trademarks in the United States, the United Kingdom, Europe and other countries.

ISBN: 978-1-137-50409-8 EPUB
ISBN: 978-1-137-50408-1 PDF
ISBN: 978-1-137-50407-4 Hardback

A catalogue record for this book is available from the British Library.

A catalog record for this book is available from the Library of Congress.

www.palgrave.com/pivot

DOI: 10.1057/9781137504081

Contents

Preface

This monograph highlights a renewed emphasis in international affairs on regional studies and geopolitics. The co-authors provide an assessment for academic and professional audiences engaged in studying and policymaking in light of the revolutionary changes in the politics and security of the Middle East and North Africa. The monograph explores the Arab Spring revolutions – in Tunisia, Egypt, Libya and Syria – and the security implications that lay at the temporal and special intersection of internal and regional dimensions of each case study. The consequences of the Arab Spring affected security in the Mediterranean, Middle East and North Africa regions that led to direct outside military interventions, either directly or indirectly, in addition to the intensive political and security engagement with all four countries. We analyze how these threats emerged, their current status, and how best to deal with them. For example, how can current governments, facing "failed, failing and fragile" states, establish effective institutions to restore state authority and push socio-economic development, all within the democratization process? How should the US, EU and NATO's policies be updated to adjust for new socio-political phenomena and threats in Mediterranean security?

Notwithstanding the entrenched lack of democracy and societal (ethnic, tribal, religious, etc.) in the region, we believe these were not the principal causes for the collapse the region is facing since the Arab Spring. Instead, we argue that it was the state failure/weakness that is the cause – the original sin – and consequently redemption should be

DOI: 10.1057/9781137504081.0002

state building. Unlike conventional, widespread wisdom on state building in the recent literature, this book advances the argument that skilled leadership and independence bureaucracy are keys to the solution no less than the central role of the United States and the European Union.

DOI: 10.1057/9781137504081.0002

Acknowledgments

The authors gratefully acknowledge Palgrave Macmillan's Palgrave Pivot publications for encouraging timely research on current events in international affairs. The efforts of Hannah Kašpar, Editorial Assistant, International Relations, have been essential in guiding this research project from its inception. The authors dedicate this Palgrave Pivot to all in the Middle East who have sacrificed so much and have committed themselves to end the ongoing wars of hatred to bring security, stability and peace to a very troubled region during a critical time in world history.

▶

DOI: 10.1057/9781137504081.0003

About the Authors

Amr Yossef is an independent scholar based in Cairo, Egypt. He holds a PhD in International Studies from the University of Trento, Italy in 2009. In the framework of his doctoral research, he has been a visiting scholar at the Bush School of Government, Texas A&M University, and the Saltzman Institute of War and Peace Studies, Columbia University. He was also a post-doctoral fellow at the Taub Center for Israel Studies, New York University (2011–2012). Yossef has previously taught at the American University in Cairo and at NYU. His publications have appeared in the *European Political Science, Digest of Middle East Studies, and Journal of Strategic Studies.*

Joseph R. Cerami, joined the Bush School of Government and Public Service at Texas A&M University in August 2001. He teaches leadership and national security studies in the Master's Program in International Affairs. He was appointed as the founding director of the Bush School's Public Service Leadership Program in 2002. Cerami taught previously at the US Military Academy at West Point, and at the US Army War College, where he served as the chair of the Department of National Security and Strategy. His book, *Leadership and Policy Innovations – From Clinton to Bush: Countering the Proliferation of Weapons of Mass Destruction* was published in 2013. In January 2016, Cerami will join the University of St. Thomas in Houston, as the Burnett Family Distinguished Chair in Leadership, and a director of the new University Center for Ethical Leadership.

palgrave▶pivot

www.palgrave.com/pivot

1

The Original Sin: The Failure of the Arab State

Abstract: *This chapter argues that the "authority vacuum" that followed the revolutions against Arab authoritarian regimes – affecting state's ability to deliver public services which influenced citizens' human and state's national security – is the symptom rather than the cause of the current turmoil. Arab populations protesting in 2011 against poverty, corruption and poor services, are now facing worse conditions than those they have protested against. The original sin is the failure/ weakness of the post-colonial Arab state in its pursuit of modernity. Arab republics, set up by revolutions/ coups in the 1950s and the 1960s, promised to establish a modern, democratic state based on socio-economic justice. Nevertheless, four decades later, Arab states were still lagging behind in economic and political development, social justice, and the provision of services. Injustices were kept silent by the heavy hand of the regimes which, once challenged or toppled, gave way to the current turmoil.*

Yossef, Amr and Joseph R. Cerami. *The Arab Spring and the Geopolitics of the Middle East: Emerging Security Threats and Revolutionary Change.* Basingstoke: Palgrave Macmillan, 2015. DOI: 10.1057/9781137504081.0005.

1.1   Legitimacy or capacity of the state?

Conventional wisdom explains the turmoil that spun out of control in the Arab world after its Spring revolutions in terms of the lack of democracy and liberal traditions in addition to the incohesivness inherent in the Arab state which is itself a novel creation by colonialism and where political identity follows tribal, ethnic, and religious lines rather than the modern, nation-state line. In essence, this wisdom resonates with the words of Elie Kedourie: "the nation-state in the Middle East is an idea that bristles with difficulties. Not only is the idea of a nation itself by no means simple and straightforward ... but also the very notion of a state is quite difficult to fit into the political thought that is traditional to the Middle East, namely, Muslim political thought."[1] This school of thought, though plausible to a certain extent, presents only a partial explanation for the events that preceded and those that followed the Arab Spring, which are strongly linked.

It is important at the outset to spell out clearly that a state's stability relies on two main pillars: *legitimacy* and *capacity*. The conventional school of thought stresses the element of legitimacy while this chapter challenges this view and stresses instead the element of capacity. This latter notion has received several definitions and expressions in the Middle East studies literature. As Joachim Ahrens put it, governance refers, in essence, to two of the most basic questions posed by political scientists "Who governs?" and "How well?" The former question concerns the issues of power and legitimacy, while the latter is concerned with good government that is associated with "effective institutions, equitable policy outcomes, capacity to adapt to changing conditions, [and] participation and satisfaction of citizens in decisions affecting them."[2]

Similarly, according to Saad Eddin Ibrahim, true representation of the society's constituencies and ambitions is a "necessary condition" for the stability of the state and the ruling regime, though "sufficient conditions" for this stability exist when the state represents institutions able to provide services, protection and fair distribution of resources.[3] In a similar vein, Nazih Ayubi wrote:

> [T]he state allocates all kinds of value in society: it allocates not only (economic) resources but also (moral) values ... This has been particularly prominent in the case of radical, populist regimes. If such states fail – as did most of Arab countries – in achieving their developmental promises, for which they claim they have allocated the society's resources, then the society's

DOI: 10.1057/9781137504081.0005

response is likely to present itself either in an attempt to appropriate from the state part of its enlarged economic domain (i.e., via privatisations) and/or in an attempt to regain part of the 'moral capital' for the direct benefit of the civil society (as represented, for example, by the Islamist groupings).[4]

Between Arab states and their populations since the 1950s existed a working "unwritten social contract" according to which the society refrains from practicing politics in return for receiving from the state several other non-political demands, in terms of services and benefits.[5] This arrangement became especially relevant after the collapse of Arab nationalism's appeal, as a legitimizing tool, following the catastrophic defeat of June 1967. In Ibrahim's view, along with oppression and political blackmail, Arab regimes employed also "efficiency in solving problems," in areas such as housing, employment and infrastructure, to enhance their legitimacy.

In this regard, the crisis in legitimacy has pushed some portions of Arab societies to give up Arab nationalism and search instead for a different reference of meaning, loyalty and legitimacy in other forms, religious, tribal, sectarian or ethnic. Given the violence that erupted in the Arab Spring countries over religious, tribal and ethnic divisions or affiliations, much ink has been spilled repeating the argument on the artificial nature of state in the Arab world in which legitimacy has always been based on these aforementioned lines rather than central, nation-state authority. This argument, however, appears to overlook three important aspects of the sub-state "divisions" in the Arab world. First, as Ilya Harik argued two decades ago challenging the well-established view, Arab countries constituted genuine, old states that go back to the 19th century or much older. Only the Fertile Crescent states (with the exception of Lebanon) were carved by the European colonial powers from the remnants of the Ottoman Empire. With the exception of Syria, the other three cases in this study (Egypt, Tunisia and Libya), which were also the first in the Arab Spring wave of revolutions, had old states within the bureaucratic-oligarchy type in which the authority was held by an urban military caste helped by an extensive administrative apparatus.[6]

The second aspect relates to the nature of these divisions' existence. Tribes, sects and ethnicities have coexisted peacefully for centuries within the territory of each of the respective Arab states which historically have not constituted a central government, nation-state authority, such as Libya and Syria. The concept of a "tribe" has often been erroneously used to refer to autonomous, uncompromising social units, loyalty to which relies solely on family and blood-ties, where in fact tribes shared some powerful unifying factors as well, particularly religion (predominantly Islam) and economic interdependence, which in themselves were usually used by the central authority as means of social and political control.[7] That is to say that the mere existence of these affiliations, even when strong as they are already so in several other regions in the world, does not inevitably replace the legitimacy of the state unless these affiliations are combined with other factors that push in this direction. In Bassem Tibi's view, the reason the Arab Middle East failed in what Europe has succeeded, that is attaining "cultural homogeneity by melding various ethnicities into single nations," is not only uneven industrialization and modernization, but also state failure:

> The newly established nation-states have failed to cope with the social and economic problems created by rapid development because they cannot provide the proper institutions to alleviate these problems. Because the nominal nation-state has not met the challenge, society has restored to its pre-national ties as a solution, thereby preserving the framework of the patron-client relationships.[8]

The final aspect relates to the observation that it was the political regimes that have contributed to maintain these divisions. Employing deliberate policies of discrimination and cooptation, these regimes instrumentalized existing tribal, ethnic and religious divisions in society in a typical divide-and-rule fashion. Dismantling the country's nascent political and economic institutions, Qaddafi started with abolishing the tribe as a legal institution and ended up making it a formal partner in the political process by establishing the so-called Social People's Leaderships within the regime's plethora of committees. However, that was neither equal nor efficient. On the one hand, the Qaddafi regime, despite the oil riches that allowed an extensive welfare system "has done little ... to foster sufficient political and economic development to guarantee that the current high standard of living will be sustainable."[9] On the other hand, the tribes that supported the regime and were used to protect it, the Qaddadfa, Warfalla and Muqarha, were economically and politically rewarded, whereas "the large number of tribes ... stayed aloof from the regime even if not necessarily acting against it. The latter were relatively marginalized and suffered economic hardship and political exclusion."[10] A clear example is Libya's East, where Qaddafi

DOI: 10.1057/9781137504081.0005

feared rebellion, that faced systematic economic underdevelopment as punishment.[11] This, in turn, resulted in having the individuals in the majority of tribes continue to depend on the tribe as the guaranteed provider and protector, therefore re-producing the old nature of the tribe as a unit for social control, social reference, and economic fulfilment, and hence political loyalty.

In Syria, the Assad regime was quite aware of the country's "communal question," and followed a policy generally successful in accommodating its various confessional groups. The seeds of the uprising, according to Eyal Zisser, seem to have been generated in the beginning of the 2000s "[when] the more inclusive, representative character and orientation of the Syrian regime declined. It even seemed as if the ruling elites had turned their back on the Sunni population in the villages and peripheral areas that had until then been its own flesh and blood."[12]

The great appeal and increasing influence of Islamism to the masses emanated from an inherent promise of modernity and development in each country. It is extremely doubtful that the Arab "man in the street" has been or is primarily preoccupied with cultural identity in and of itself as the issue to which he/she would dedicate himself/herself, unless in extreme cases such as foreign occupation or total war. As an ideology, however, Islamism is similar to Arab nationalism, local-national ideologies and socialism that have been mostly the concerns of elites and have hardly penetrated the masses, usually undeveloped communities, in the Arab world. Inherent in "culturalism," the exacerbation of ideological, religious or other identities in the Arab world grossly overlooks the heterogeneous and constantly transformed nature of any group configuration, only to draw "lethal power from the assumption that a so-called 'cultural identity'... corresponds to a 'political identity.'"[13] In this regard, the invocation of ideological identifies as the source of political action in the current Middle East conflagrations is only reminiscent of the Thirty Years' War in Europe (1618–1648) where "sectarian alignments were invoked for solidarity and motivation in battle but were just as often discarded, trumped by clashes of geopolitical interests or simply the ambitions of outsized personalities."[14]

The real questions for the vast majority of citizens have always been and still are, not "who rules?" or "who are we?" but rather "how are we?" and "how well?" Endeavouring to define "a strong state" in Arab

DOI: 10.1057/9781137504081.0005

context, Gassan Salamé noticed that "Ibn Khaldun judiciously distinguishes between two ingredients of the state's strength. There are, on the one hand, the actual capabilities of the state and, on the other, the recognition by others [in the society] of these capabilities," showing that whether it was nationalism, Islamism, or even the military ascendance to power, these were all, in the end, attempts to overcome long-time underdevelopment and reach strength.[15]

In the same vein, Islamism would not have been able to survive and mobilize had it not been for the social role it played in terms of supplying many types of social services that the state has also failed to sufficiently deliver. Under Sadat and Mubarak in Egypt, "The rise of social welfare institutions demonstrates that the Muslim Brotherhood emerged as a direct competitor to the state in the provision of services that are a direct extension of the state's domain."[16] That is to imply that the capacity of the state played no less role than the ideological tools of legitimacy in maintaining or threatening the stability of the Arab state. The "unwritten social contract" that apparently worked for decades, was no longer valid in 2011, partly because of the deterioration in state legitimacy but more importantly because of the deterioration of its capacity. Similarly, strained by population growth and inefficient economic structures, the Assad regime in Syria started to tolerate, starting from the late 1990s, a wide network of charitable activities by Islamists (especially Jamat Zayd, a Sufi-inspired but politically aware Islamic organization).[17]

This is neither to say that political freedoms did not matter for the Arab populace, nor to endorse the argument of Arab authoritarian regimes that the Arabs are not qualified for democracy and/or that economic development should necessarily take priority over political reform. Rather, we argue that the main motivation of the masses to join the intelligentsia, forming a critical mass to challenge the long-ruling regimes was to protest against the failure of the state to provide – that is, the state capacity, rather than the legitimacy of the state political system or democracy. For instance, Lindsay Benstead, using the same Arab Barometer data from six nations in the years 2006–2008 that offer ample evidence of support for democracy in the Arab world, found that 72% of Arabs support democracy in general but see it as unsuitable for their country. In particular, Benstead concluded that "beliefs that democracy will have negative consequences and perceptions of poor government performance are the most important predictors of democracy's unsuitability."[18]

DOI: 10.1057/9781137504081.0005

The citizens' primary concern with government performance is evident in that in Hosni Mubarak's last year of rule in Egypt, not only did public satisfaction with economic prospect fall, but also there was a greater stress on the shortcomings of the state. On the revolution eve, in 2010 according to a Gallup poll, there were dramatic declines in the rates of satisfaction with government services in Egypt and Tunisia as compared with 2009.[19] Noticeably, public satisfaction with government services went much lower even under democratically-elected governments in Egypt, Tunisia and Libya in 2013.[20]

In other words, the support of the masses to the uprisings was akin to the following complaint of a young Iranian woman in a letter to a daily in July 1980: "[During the revolution], I used to think revolution meant clothing and covering bare feet of the poor. I thought it meant feeding the hungry. Now I know how optimistic I was ... Because neither my bare feet are covered, nor my hunger is satisfied."[21] Twenty-three years later, Egyptian columnist Gamal Abul Hassan echoed in writing:

> It is true that January [revolution] advocated the slogan of democracy, but most of those who advocated it had no idea how this complex system functions. Most of them envisioned a system similar to the one that decided to execute Socrates 2500 years ago, that is, a simple system that allows the majority to express its views and to elect its rulers. January, in essence, was an upheaval for dignity, not democracy. Dignity, unlike democracy, is an apolitical concept. It rather means that people want to feel self-respect and have a decent life. All of this is unrelated to democracy, this complex system that depends, in principle, on the checks-and-balances and the strength of institutions.[22]

This argument receives support from the fact that two years after the revolutions, Egyptians, for example, are far more likely to support military rule than people in many other Middle East countries. More than seven out of ten Egyptians say it is good to have the army rule – a much larger figure than that in Iraq, Lebanon, Pakistan, Tunisia or Turkey.[23] Testimony to this is the fact that Egyptians and Tunisians ended up electing in 2014 two presidents, Abdel Fatah Sisi and Beji Caid Essebsi, respectively, who both stressed in their campaigns restoring *haybat al-dawla* (the fear/respect of state) and the "strong state", requesting from their populations a "mandate" to eradicate terrorism. In Syria, by 2012 some 55% of Syrians wanted President Bashar Assad to stay, motivated by fear of civil war,[24] and in 2014 there was a clear majority (71%) that thinks that the Assad government will remain at least for the coming three years, while 35% said that the Assad government best represents the true interest of the Syrian people.[25]

DOI: 10.1057/9781137504081.0005

1.2   The "how well?" question

Following the eruption of revolutions against authoritarian regimes in Tunisia, Egypt, Libya and Syria in 2011, these Arab Spring countries have all witnessed, to different degrees, what can be called a vacuum of authority, a severe deterioration of the state's ability to deliver public services which influenced citizens' human security and state's national security. The Arab populations protesting in 2011 against poverty, corruption and poor services, are now facing even worse conditions than those they have protested against.

Facing these Arab states and societies is the core problem – that we call the "original sin" – that has accompanied the Arab modern state since its inception and, as we will show in greater detail below. The original sin is the weakness or failure of the post-colonial Arab state in its pursuit of modernity. Arab republics, set up by revolutions/coups in the 1950s and the 1960s, promised a modern, democratic state based on socio-economic justice. Nevertheless, four decades later, the Arab state was relatively still lagging behind in economic and political development, social justice, and the provision of health, education and rule of law. Injustices were kept silent by the heavy hand of the authoritarian regimes which, once challenged or toppled, gave way to the current turmoil, though the degree to which this turmoil developed depended on each country's specific characteristics.

The failure of the Arab state before, but especially after, the Arab Spring revolutions, is something that most take for granted. Nevertheless, much attention has been paid thus far to investigate the sources of this failure as a result of authoritarianism and the lack of democratic governments but much less from the perspective of the state as an organizational structure – that is, institutions – and to link the impact of this failure to the developments of the Arab Spring. Two definitions are important here: the state and state strength. William Zartman once proposed the following components of state strength: stability, capacity, security, autonomy, accountability and legitimacy.[26] Nevertheless, these components unduly confuse not only between state capacity and legitimacy but also confuse between the constituents of state strength and its outcome – stability.

We adopt Joel Migdal's functional definition of the state as "an organization, composed of numerous agencies led and coordinated by the state's leadership (executive authority) that has the ability or authority to make and implement the binding rules for all the people as well as the parameters of rule making for other social organizations in a given territory, using force if necessary to have its way."[27] Also, in Joel Migdal's view, a state strength is:

> [A]bout the capabilities of states to achieve the kinds of changes in society that their leaders have sought through state planning, policies and actions. Capabilities include the capacities to penetrate society, regulate social relationships, extract resources, and appropriate or use resources in determined ways. Strong states are those with high abilities to complete these tasks, while weak states are on the low end of a spectrum of capabilities.[28]

In the same vein, Francis Fukuyama defines a state's strength as "the ability to enact statutes and to frame and execute policies; to administer the public business with relative efficiency; to control graft, corruption, and bribery; to maintain high levels of transparency and accountability in governmental institutions; and most importantly, to *enforce* laws."[29] Similarly, in the words of Lisa Anderson, "states whose modern administrative structures are well-established and stable are termed 'strong', [whereas] those administrations that are either incapable of consistently reaching the major part of the population in order to extract resources and provide services or are characterized by patrimonial patterns of recruitment and operations are 'weak.'"[30]

In this regard, very few of the Arab states have been or are strong states. The "hard" nature of the Arab state – manifested in the huge coercive security apparatus that the authoritarian regimes, nationalistic or Islamist, possessed to quell internal conflict, oppress opposition and preserve themselves (discussed in greater detail in Chapter 2) – should not be confused with the "strong" nature of the state's governance which is related to the institutional capacity, particularly law enforcement and administrative efficiency, with the notable example of taxation capacity. This is what Ayubi has termed the "fierce" state that is "often violent *because* it is weak," that is, the state's despotic power is great only when the government can act arbitrarily, but is little when it comes to translating orders into law enforcement or implementing development plans.[31]

The literature on the failure of the Arab state in achieving development attributes all but explains the weakness or the failure of the state by the authoritarian nature of the Arab regimes. In this, the literature draws heavily on democratic theory. On the one hand, there are the

DOI: 10.1057/9781137504081.0005

institutional constraints of democracies. Through fair elections and other forms of checks-and-balances, democratic governments are both representative of and accountable to their peoples. Since democratic leaders want to be re-elected, they will be careful to achieve tangible successes and fulfil their electoral promises, lest, in case they fail in doing so, they lose office in next elections. That is in contrast to autocratic leaders who are answerable only to themselves. Consequently, autocrats care less about achieving development since the populace is not empowered to punish them for failing to do so; dictators are unlikely to fall from power, unless by a military coup or a popular revolution. On the other hand, there is organizational effectiveness. In other words, appointments that depend on professionalism rather than loyalties and a democratic political culture that encourages accountability rather than corruption, all produce efficient bureaucrats with high levels of leadership and initiative. This is in contrast to bureaucracies of authoritarian regimes that are dedicated to safeguarding the privileges of those in power, and therefore into self-serving, unaccountable and corrupt machines that lack effectiveness and innovation.

While the undemocratic nature of the Arab state is undeniable, the above explanations appear to be obsessed with the "fierce" nature of the Arab state as an explanatory variable. However, to assign all the Arab state's ills on the lack of democracy is not only unrealistic but it is also misleading.

First, it is unrealistic because democracy is not an automatic path to state strength or development. For example, as of 2013, out of 94 states that are the lowest in the World Bank's Country Policy and Institutional Assessment (CPIA) score-card to measure governance performance,[32] almost a third (27 states) are defined as democratic according to POLITY IV Project data set developed to measure the level of democracy in a state.[33] It should come as no surprise, then, that, reviewing 141 states in the *Index of State Weakness in the Developing World*, Susan Rice and Steward Patrick stated that "[a]lthough the majority of the critically weak and weak states falter in the political sphere, democratic governance is not always associated with strong state capacity."[34] A notable example is India, the world's largest democracy, where the state ability to enforce laws and deliver services is highly questionable in large parts of the country. In addition, to expect these countries to turn into liberal democracies *a la* Western model would take generations, and the recent experience of Iraq and the post-Arab Spring countries is a telling example.

DOI: 10.1057/9781137504081.0005

Second, this explanation is misleading because it incorrectly equates democracy with liberal political culture and law enforcement. Democracy is different from both; a state can be an "electoral democracy" without a liberal social order advancing individualism (such as Hungary), and a state can also be a strong law enforcer (such as China) without necessarily being democratic. As we have argued earlier, state weakness/failure – against which Arab populations revolted – has not been the result of a lack of democracy. Indeed, it might very well be the other way around. Examining the evolution and development of state institutions in Tunisia and Libya in the nineteenth and twentieth centuries, Anderson found that the variation in these two countries political systems – that is Tunisia's attributes of Western-inspired parliamentary democracy and Libya's military takeover and revolutionary upheaval – is explained by the "presence or absence of a stable administration." That is, according to Anderson, "not only because bureaucracy is a powerful instrument for the development, coordination, and application of policy, but because the very existence of a stable administration determines much of the character of political organization and social structure."[35]

Accordingly, the weakness or failure of the Arab states is due neither to the lack of financial resources nor to the influence of authoritarian policies, though both obviously had an impact. It is rather a reflection of the weakness of its bureaucracy – its stateness. Despite the common announcement of huge development plans, the Arab state has failed to deliver development to their societies. The reason why the bureaucracy has been weak is the *absence of a mission*, that is, that the political leaders have typically failed to give the bureaucracy proper direction. In the absence of a mission, little serious, methodical planning takes place, despite the fact that the Arab ministers and director-generals have predominantly been chosen among the technocrats with supposedly sufficient expertise in the ministry or state agency they are managing, a fact that indicates that the absence of a mission has not been the exclusive responsibility of the political leaderships. In the absence of planning, no proper professional qualification is assigned to bureaucrats, whose majority is the product of a public education system (at school and university levels alike) that has usually been outdated, unrelated to the needs of job market, and, above all, hinders concepts of change or development.[36]

DOI: 10.1057/9781137504081.0005

Much like the education system adopted a "more-of-the-same" approach, little innovation is allowed, and little effectiveness is achieved by bureaucrats, who, despite all modern and formal appearances, used to learn about their jobs less by training and more by tradition from their elder colleagues, and engage in their profession less by law and operational procedures and more by the tradition of "how-things-go." Here it is important to note that out of the enormous intellectual, talented and skilled Arab youth, few of these work in state agencies and even fewer of them get the chance, if at all, to make any significant difference in their work place. This then is also why very few state bureaucrats, from those at the tops of government agencies to implementers in the field, apparently have any idea what is the design they are supposed to carry out nor received the necessary training. Therefore, the Arab governments rarely had at their disposal experienced and effective bureaucracies that are capable of properly governing a country.

The wide expansion of Arab bureaucracies – in the number of administrative units, the number of public employees, the increase in government expenditures, and the increase in the salaries of these employees – as one symptom of the "rentier" nature of the Arab state (oil riches or worker remittances), did not help a lot but rather constituted an obstacle to development.[37] Instead, Arab populace received the well-known "ills of bureaucracy" :

1   Public organizations are overstaffed, employees are underpaid and productivity is low.
2   Innovative and effective public managers are in short supply.
3   Centralized decision-making and nepotism that can affect even relatively successful systems.
4   Severe troublesome problems, especially "increased red-tape," "lack of authority to make decisions," "indecisiveness and avoidance of risk," and "government interference in business affairs."
5   Corruption that involves bribery and misuse of authority for personal gain.
6   Arab administrative structures, mirroring the political context, have not adapted to the urgent need for inclusionary decision-making processes.[38]

Each of these ills seems to support the other. For example, corruption, that is the common antitheses of reform but does not elicit the necessary

DOI: 10.1057/9781137504081.0005

legal punishment, is itself blamed on "poor pay, inadequate fringe bene-fits, weak commitment to the state or the party in power, lack of moni-toring and control, and the culture of the society."[39] Similarly, corruption, combined with crippling labor laws and centralized decision-making, bring about a failure to impose adequate discipline and to take action or implement policies as planned or in due time. The unfortunate result is that a large number of unqualified personnel are running a country. Since these bureaucrats cannot perform what they are there for, that is, delivery of service, bureaucratic politics takes precedence – fighting over resources and influence, personal feuds and power conflicts, which makes the institutions they belong to unready to fulfil their raison d'être. A major manifestation of the Arab state failure is the repeated pattern of sudden collapse of Arab militaries in battle. According to Abul Hassan:

> It cannot be that Palestinians, Egyptians and Iraqis are cowards. There must be another explanation for the collapse of Arab armies in these confronta-tions... The key [to success] is not about sophisticated equipment or the bravery of men. It rather lies in the ability to organize people and managing them in a methodical way. That is called 'institutions,' that is something that the modern Arab states had not known except in appearance and pour la forme.[40]

Some have argued quite the opposite. Explaining the outbreak of the Arab Spring revolutions, Ibrahim Elnur opined that "[T]he authoritar-ian regimes based on political patronage in the Middle East generated the seeds of their own dissolution, not through failure to deliver, but *precisely* because they succeeded in delivering the patronage package [from education to various other manifestations of modernity], albeit with diverse degrees of success."[41] This view is oversimplified. That is because the increase in size is not always translated into quality and, more importantly, to being a developed country, not the least because of the essential difference in how to define a state strength/weakness and its success/failure. In the words of Fukuyama,

> It therefore makes sense to distinguish between the *scope* of state activities, which refers to the different functions and goals taken on by governments, and the *strength* of state power, which has to do with the ability of states to plan and execute policies, and to enforce laws cleanly and transparently – what is now commonly referred to as state or institutional capacity.[42]

This difference explains, for example, why the Arab states have achieved relatively some progress in the socio-economic indicators, that is the

DOI: 10.1057/9781137504081.0005

scope of state activities (Table 1.1), but score poorly when it comes to the strength of state power, that is government effectiveness, regulatory quality, rule of law, and control of corruption (Table 1.2).

TABLE 1.1   *Major socioeconomic indicators in Arab Spring countries, 2010*

	Human Development Index (country ranking)	Human Development Index	Life Expectancy (years)	Mean Schooling (years)	Gross National Income per Capita (US$)	Gender Inequality Index (country ranking)	Adult Literacy (%, age 15+)
Libya	53	0.755	74.5	7.3	17,078	52	88.4
Tunisia	81	0.683	74.3	6.5	7,977	56	78.0
Egypt	101	0.626	70.5	6.5	5,889	108	66.4
Syria	111	0.589	74.6	4.9	4,670	103	83.6

Source: United Nations Development Program, *Human Development Report 2010* http://hdr.undp.org/en/content/human-development-report-2010.

TABLE 1.2   *Governance indicators in Arab Spring countries, 2010 (scores out of 100)*

	Government Effectiveness	Regulatory Quality	Rule of Law	Control of Corruption
Libya	12.9	9.6	19.0	5.2
Tunisia	63.2	53.1	59.7	54.8
Egypt	43.1	46.9	51.2	34.3
Syria	32.5	20.6	36.5	12.9

Source: The World Bank, *The Worldwide Governance Indicators Project, 1996–2013* http://info.worldbank.org/governance/wgi/index.aspx#home.

TABLE 1.3   *Progress with structural reform in Arab Spring countries*

	Governance: Quality of Administration	Governance: Public Sector Accountability
Libya	4	0
Tunisia	73	20
Egypt	42	23
Syria	13	8

Note: A country's current status reflects its 2007 placement in a worldwide ordering based on a variety of indicators, with 100 reflecting the country with the best policies (and the greatest improvements), and 0 the country with the worst policies (and the greatest deterioration).

Source: The World Bank, *MENA Region Economic Developments and Prospects, 2008.*

DOI: 10.1057/9781137504081.0005

The bureaucracy's performance, we argue, has been the key to the weakness of the state and its ability to deliver. Max Weber is often cited to refer to the failure of the post-Arab Spring states to form an organization "[whose] administrative staff successfully upholds a claim to the *monopoly of legitimate* use of physical force in the enforcement of its order ... within a given *territorial* area."[43] Nevertheless, Weber is under-represented when it comes to the function and structure of this administrative staff which stressed the following elements: division of labor based on functional specialization, hierarchy of authority (legal and rational), rule-set rights and obligations, written rules and procedures, impersonal relations, and staffing based on technical competence.

One need not be an expert to know that Arab bureaucracies could be anything but efficient or even close to these requirements, which explains the lack of development. Analyzing 35 less developed countries, including Egypt, Syria and Tunisia, James Rauch and Peter Evans have shown that structural features (competitive salaries, internal promotion and career stability, and meritocratic recruitment) constitute the key ingredients of effective state bureaucracies and, in turn, could predict a country's economic performance.[44] Similarly, analyzing several countries in the Middle East, John Merriam has also concluded that bureaucrats were failed agents of development in the region.[45] According to the UN *Arab Development Report* 2002:

> Arab countries as a group fall below the world average on all [quality of institutions] indicators ... except that of the rule of law, where they only marginally exceed the average. Subdividing Arab countries on the basis of the UNDP HDI [Human Development Index] classification of high, medium and low human development [findings show] that the high human-development group of Arab countries enjoys above-average quality of institutions for all indicators except 'voice and accountability.'[46]

The state weakness in the four Arab Spring countries varied among them so that they can be put in the following order of strength: Tunisia, Egypt, Syria and Libya. Nevertheless, all of them fell in the "weak state" category. For example, in the *Index of State Weakness in the Developing World*, Egypt, Syria and Libya were all under the set "States to Watch" – "because of their significant weakness in particular areas and thus their potential to exhibit increased overall fragility," as their overall rankings, out of 141 states, were 78, 59 and 86 respectively. Only Tunisia fared significantly better as it scored 112.[47]

DOI: 10.1057/9781137504081.0005

Unlike the democracy variable, which does not appear to be significantly different in these four countries,[48] the "stateness" variable we propose accounts for the variation in these countries' different paths after four years of the uprising, which is quite consistent with the variation in the governance indicators (Table 1.2). Comparatively, the cases of Tunisia and Libya are quite revealing. In post-independence era, both were governed by authoritarian regimes, though their level of "stateness" varied significantly, where Tunisia exhibited attributes of a relatively stronger state than that of Libya. The two countries also varied significantly in the paths they have taken following the fall of their respective authoritarian regimes.

The state weakness or failure in these four Arab countries has been the result of historical processes, particularly throughout the 19th and 20th centuries, that inhibited the establishment and sustainment of strong state institutions as following:

1.3   The Arab Spring countries

1.3.1   Egypt

Widely acclaimed as the example of "stateness" in the region with one of the oldest, if not the oldest, central government in history and even referred to as having a "deep state," Egypt represents nevertheless a weak state. Imitating European powers, Mohamed Ali established in Egypt in the first quarter of the 19th century a modern state that had the bureaucratic structure and administration with the capacity to mobilize resources and plan and implement wide development plans. Notably, Mohamed Ali's state was established neither on democratic governance nor national cohesion for the Egyptians it claimed to represent.[49]

This state survived up until the end of Mohamed Ali's family rule in 1952, and took advantage of the bureaucratic improvements that the British inserted since their occupation of the country in 1882. However, the state that Gamal Abdel Nasser led since 1954 was a completely different one, emphasizing the enlargement of the state activity in almost every sphere of life of Egyptians. As Migdal has shown in his *Strong Societies and Weak States*, even under Nasser's *mukhabarat* state, the government agencies were not able to transform the Egyptian society, particularly the land reform, as a way of establishing a new social and political order in the country. To be fair, two of Migdal's sufficient

DOI: 10.1057/9781137504081.0005

conditions for a strong state, that is, world historical timing and military threat, could not be controlled by Nasser, though he missed a third, a skilful leadership, and obviously downgraded the fourth – an independent bureaucracy of people who are "skilful enough to execute the grand designs of state leaders."[50]

The wide expansion of bureaucracy under Nasser, Sadat and Mubarak, did little to improve the government capacity. The provision of services has increasingly taken on a surrealistic quality where the sheer size and impressive appearance of state institutions, with the exception of the security services, ostensibly implied that serious work is being done and public goods are indeed being delivered sufficiently, while in fact little is being done or sufficiently delivered. In what Samer Soliman called "the paradox of the weak state and the strong regime," the ability of the Egyptian state under Mubarak fell dramatically, a phenomenon that could be observed not only in the deterioration of public services (education, health, transportation, etc.) but also, and perhaps more importantly, in law enforcement. Large violent disputes (either between big families/tribes in rural Egypt or between Muslims and Christians) were settled out of the judicial system and rather mediated through the state's security services. Other examples include the inability of the state to prevent the massive illegal seizure of state lands or the illegal construction on agricultural, though private, lands and the feeble response of state agencies to the wide breach of urban-planning codes that resulted in the emergence of mass of neighbourhoods, in almost every city, if not of slum houses, that lack the requisite infrastructure services.

1.3.2   Syria

Assad's Syria is perhaps the typical example of Ayubi's "fierce state" with its notorious security services that have been effectively running the country's affairs for decades. However, much like Egypt, this did not mean having a strong state that can fulfil policy tasks. Though Hafez Assad managed to construct a containment system "that aligned the interests of most social groups with his government," it never managed to develop "the type of accountable institutions and productive economic activity necessary."[51] As early as the 1990s, this form of class-inclusive, authoritarian-corporatist polity has exhausted the Syrian state that started then to retreat, giving off some of its responsibilities to civil society.

DOI: 10.1057/9781137504081.0005

A similar reality was repeated in the early 2000s, under Bashar Assad. Having initiated economic liberalization after years of socialist austerity, Bashar encouraged an administrative reform recognizing that "over-centralization is a severe problem [where] there is little a civil servant below the rank of minister can decide," and the main reform agenda included training and retaining cadres on the one hand, and encouraging ministers to delegate authority, appoint advisors and issue clear job descriptions.[52] All this failed and Syrians were left with "the institutional weakness of the 'vast, lethargic bureaucracy'... [under] a shortage of competent technocrats, ineffective courts, and widespread corruption."[53] The failure of public administration reforms has "forced the consideration of other policy alternatives in which the state is not the centrepiece," giving greater reliance on private initiatives.[54] The most telling example is that the government lacked any response to the devastating 2006–2010 drought, which filled burgeoning slums with 1.5 million people, mostly Sunni peasants.[55]

1.3.3   Libya

In the first quarter of the 19th century, the garrison state in Libya initiated "defensive modernization," in response to the rising threat from Europe, military superiority in the Mediterranean and the diversion of the sub-Saharan trade to the Atlantic. On the eve of Italian invasion in 1911, Libya did have stable public administration penetrating into the hinterlands, both on the monopoly of the use of force and taxation. Nevertheless, because the Libyan leadership obeyed the Ottomans in opposing the Italians, the latter chose to destroy the nascent Libyan administration and replace it with one of their own that was disorganized and inefficient, even by the relatively low Ottoman standards of the Ottoman bureaucracy.[56]After independence, the Sanusi monarchy drew heavily on the tribes partly because the "domestic population [was] skeptical of the utility and reliability of bureaucratic administration and commercial exchange."[57]

Following the 1969 coup and throughout the 1970s, Qadafi pursued a radical socio-economic restructuring of Libya. That was accompanied by the weakening of tribal notables, first by abolishing the tribe as a legal institution and re-drawing of the boundaries of local administrative units, which had been based on tribal territories and then by initiating a wide distribution of the oil revenue that offered free education, housing, medical care, and transportation, to replace tribal and kinship allegiances with that of the regime that permitted access to goods and services.

DOI: 10.1057/9781137504081.0005

Nevertheless, Qaddafi's welfare state appropriately delivered little in either direction. Precisely because welfare "distributive policies demand relatively little by way of an efficient bureaucracy,"[58] tribal affiliations had been revived in the face of virtually no state and no government. Qaddafi's solution to the fear of the return of the exploiting state "was a denial that such a state is necessary and a declaration that the people supervise themselves in the *jamahiriyyah*."[59] In 2003, Qaddafi already stated that public sector had failed, because "administration is the source of corruption," and should be abolished, and therefore called for the privatization of the oil industry and the direct distribution of the oil revenues. According to Wolfram Lacher, "deliberate strategies to weaken state institutions prompted recourse to tribal networks, including in dispute settlement."[60] Consequently, Qaddafi ended up with the re-establishment of the tribal notables formally in governing structure through the Social People's Committees.

According to Anderson, "prolonged failure to develop a stable state administration not only hinders state capacity to mobilize resources domestically, a weakness whose deleterious consequences will presumably become manifest as oil revenues decline, but also inhibits formulation and implementation of development."[61] Having deliberately weakened state institutions, which were effectively replaced by a confusing patchwork of networks (such as the Popular Committees) with unclear and overlapping responsibilities,[62] there was little hope of pursuing development even with the oil riches. In fact, "the majority of population lived in on a combination of badly paid public-sector jobs and subsidies, with young people being particularly affected by widespread unemployment. Consequently... income differences among the majority of population remained small."[63] A telling example is the Toubou ethnicity, around 350,000 people in the south, whose members have suffered decades-long marginalization, denied access to services, such as education and healthcare, and even stripped of their Libyan citizenship, so that several of them under these severe socio-economic conditions turned into illegal activities, especially trafficking of arms and narcotics.

1.3.4   Tunisia

Like Libya, the garrison state in Tunisia in the first quarter of the 19th century initiated "defensive modernization," in response to the rising European military and trade threats. On the eve of French invasion in 1881, Tunisia had stable public administration reaching well into the

DOI: 10.1057/9781137504081.0005

hinterlands, both on the monopoly of the use of force and taxation. Unlike Libya, however, obedience to the Bey meant submission to the French, which helped the latter in strengthening and accelerating the Tunisian state bureaucratic control.[64]

That helps understand why Tunisia fared much better than the three other Arab Spring countries in its "stateness," as Habib Bourgiba built upon the French administration to consolidate the Tunisian state. Despite the lack of democratic governance, it remained, relatively, "an orderly society with a strong bureaucratic tradition, considerable degree of social tolerance, and emphasis on the rule of law."[65] Nevertheless, by the end of Zine El Abidine Ben-Ali's tenure, the state was still unable to confront the double-problem of high unemployment, that reached 14% by modest government estimates, and the rising of prices, along with the decrease in the revenue of Tunisian expatriates' remittances. This was precisely the result of the established rentier-state economy, further strengthened by an over-focus on tourism and real-estate development, within neoliberal economic policy that has badly affected Tunisia since the world economic crisis in 2009. The crisis in Tunisia was caused not by an incompetent bureaucracy, but essentially by misguided economic development strategy. This is a situation that looks much like Algeria in the 1980s, in that "the shift of the state focus from development to crisis management was not caused by an incompetent bureaucracy which lacked training and skills. Rather, it was brought about by the high cost of reliance on heavy industry, modern technology transfer and a sharp decline in oil prices."[66]

The relatively stronger state notwithstanding, the Tunisian government failed to provide an even development in the country's regions, as it gave preference to the north (Mediterranean coast) at the expense of the south (mostly desert). According to one Tunisian account:

> Notwithstanding the improved administration after independence, municipalities were crippled with several 'supervisions' from above. Development in Tunisia's six 'development regions' was uneven, where the three internal regions (western center, eastern south, and western south) are the least developed and characterized by high poverty, high youth unemployment, and weak infrastructure, since the state has simply given up its role in these regions.[67]

Social welfare and public service projects – hospitals, roads, sanitation services, communications and schools – were largely concentrated in the capital city and the major towns in the *Sahil* area rather than the hinterlands in the center and the south, in which Sidi Bouzid, the city were the self-immolation of Mohamed Boazizi took place, is located.

DOI: 10.1057/9781137504081.0005

The Tunisian "periphery," though in fact it constitutes almost half of the country, suffers from almost a complete, decades-long absence of the state that, according to some estimates, unemployment had reached 75% of the working-age population, while the majority of people there lives in slum houses that lack the basic infrastructure.[68]

Notes

1   Elie Kedourie, "The nation-state in the Middle East," *The Jerusalem Journal of International Relations* 9, no. 3 (1987): 1–9.

2   Cited in Jamil E Jerisat, "The Arab World: Reform or Stalemate," *Journal of Asian and African Studies* 41, no. 5/6 (October 2006): 420.

3   Saad Eddin Ibrahim et al., *Mustaqbal al-mujtama' wa al-dawla fi al-watan al-Arabi* [The Future of Society and State in the Arab Homeland] (Amman: Arab Thought Forum, 1988), p. 49.

4   Nazih Ayubi, *Over-stating the Arab state: Politics and Society in the Middle East* (London : I.B. Tauris, 1995), p. 453.

5   Ibrahim *et al.*, *Mustaqbal al-mujtama' wa al-dawla*, p. 301–302.

6   Ilya Harik, "The Origins of the Arab State System," in Gassan Salame, *The Foundations of the Arab State* (London: Routledge, 1987): pp. 19–46.

7   Ibrahim *et al.*, *Mustaqbal al-mujtama' wa al-dawla*, pp. 109–112.

8   Tibi, "The Simultaneity of the Unsimultaneous: Old Tribes and Imposed Nation-States in the Modern Middle East," in Philip S. Khoury and Joseph Kostiner, *Tribes and State Formation in the Middle East* (London: I.B. Tauris & Co Ltd. Publishers, 1990): pp. 148–149.

9   Lisa Anderson, "Tribe and State: Libyan Anomalies," in Philip S. Khoury and Joseph Kostiner, *Tribes and State Formation in the Middle East* (London: I.B. Tauris & Co Ltd. Publishers, 1990): p. 300.

10 Yehudit Ronen, "The Libyan 'Arab Spring' and Its Aftermath," in Brandon Friedman and Bruce Maddy-Weitzman, *Inglorious Revolutions: State Cohesion in the Middle East after the Arab Spring* (Tel Aviv: Moshe Dayan Center, 2014), p. 246.

11 International Crisis Group, "Popular Protest in North Africa and the Middle East (V): Making Sense of Libya," p. 18.

12 Eyal Zisser, "Syria: Between Dar'a and Suwayda: Communities and State in the Shadow of the Syrian Revolution," in Friedman and Maddy-Weitzman, *Inglorious Revolutions*, pp. 110–111.

13 Jean-François Bayrat, *The Illusion of Cultural Identity* (Chicago: University of Chicago Press 2005), p. ix.

14 Henry Kissinger, *World Order: Reflections on the Character of Nations and the Course of History* (London and New York: Allen Lane, 2014), pp. 25–26.

DOI: 10.1057/9781137504081.0005

15   Gassan Salamé, " 'Strong' and 'Weak' States, a Qualified Return to the
     Muqaddimah," in ed., *The Foundations of the Arab State* (London: Rutledge,
     1987), pp. 205–240.
16   Abdullah Al-Arian, "A State Without a State: The Egyptian Muslim
     Brotherhood's Social Welfare Institutions," *Project on Middle East Political
     Science*, no. 9, October 15, 2014: p. 8.
17   Thomas Pierret and Kjetil Selvik, "Limits of 'Authoritarian Upgrading'
     in Syria: Private Welfare, Islamic Charities, and the Rise of the Zayd
     Movement," *International Journal of Middle East Studies* 41, no. 4 (November
     2009): pp. 595–614.
18   Lindsay J. Benstead "Why do some Arab citizens see democracy as
     unsuitable for their country?", *Democratization* (ahead-of-print, 2014): p. 1
19   In Egypt, this included deterioration of satisfaction with transportation
     systems (a drop of 30%, from 78% to 48%), environment preservation (a
     drop of 15%) from 41% to 26%), affordable housing (a drop of 14% from
     39% to 26%), and education system (a drop of 5% from 61% to 56%);
     "Egypt: The Arithmetic of Revolution": http://www.gallup.com/poll/157043/
     egypt-arithmetic-revolution.aspx. In Tunisia, citizens' satisfaction with basic
     infrastructure, the cost of living, and basic services dropped noticeably in
     2010 as compared with 2009: transportation systems (a drop of 9%, from
     59% to 50%), healthcare (a drop of 20% from 71% to 51%), affordable housing
     (a drop of 33% from 74% to 41%), and education system (a drop of 6% from
     73% to 67%); "Tunisia: Analyzing the Dawn of the Arab Spring": http://www.
     gallup.com/poll/157049/tunisia-analyzing-dawn-arab-spring.aspx.
20   In Egypt, 80% of citizens saw their country as worse off, and 50% believed
     their country will still be worse off in five years, while 69% disapproved of
     the job performance of the government; "Egyptians' Views of Government
     Crashed Before Overthrow": http://www.gallup.com/poll/163796/egyptian-
     views-government-crashed-overthrow.aspx. In Tunisia, 68% of citizens
     disapproved of the job performance of the government, while 59% (down
     from 77% in 2010) said that they are living comfortably or at least getting
     by on their present incomes; "Tunisians Lose Confidence in Government":
     http://www.gallup.com/poll/163943/tunisians-lose-confidence-government.
     aspx. In Libya, 60% of citizens were dissatisfied with the performance of the
     General National Council, while 41% believed that the country is now worse
     off than before the revolution and 26% think it is about the same; National
     Democratic Institute, "Seeking Security: Public Opinion Survey in Libya,"
     Nov. 2013, https://www.ndi.org/node/20905.
21   Cited in Nimeye Digar, no. 11, 1990, pp. 114–115. https://www.h-net.
     org/~bahai/iranlib/M-R/N/nimih/ndtitle/nimih11.htm.
22   Gamal Abul Hassan "Democracy isn't an innocent angel," *Al-Masry Al-Youm*,
     August 19, 2013, http://www.almasryalyoum.com/news/details/199496.

DOI: 10.1057/9781137504081.0005

23 "Military rule popular with Egyptians": http://edition.cnn.com/2014/01/14/world/meast/egypt-military-rule/.

24 "Most Syrians back President Assad": http://www.theguardian.com/commentisfree/2012/jan/17/syrians-support-assad-western-propaganda.

25 ORB International, Face-to-Face National Opinion Poll in Syria, May 2014, http://www.orb-international.com/article.php?s=three-in-five-syrians-support-international-military-involvement.

26 I. William Zartman, "State-Building and the Military in Arab Africa," in Bahgat Korany, Paul Noble and Rex Brynen, ed., *The Many Faces of National Security in the Arab World* (London: Palgrave Macmillan, 1993), pp. 241–242.

27 Joel S. Migdal, *Strong Societies and Weak States: State-Society Relations and State Capabilities in the Third World* (Princeton, NJ: Princeton University Press, 1988), p. 19.

28 *Ibid.*, pp. 4–5.

29 Francis Fukuyama, "The Imperative of State-Building," *Journal of Democracy* 15, no. 2 (April 2004), p. 22.

30 Lisa Anderson, "The State in the Middle East and North Africa," *Comparative Politics* 20, no. 1 (October 1987): p. 2.

31 Ayubi, *Over-stating the Arab State*, pp. 449–450.

32 World Bank Country Policy and Institutional Assessment: http://databank.worldbank.org/data/views/variableselection/selectvariables.aspx?source=country-policy-and-institutional-assessment.

33 Monty G. Marshal *et al.*, Polity IV Project: Political Regime Characteristics and Transitions, 1800–2013: http://www.systemicpeace.org/polity/polity4.htm.

34 Susan E. Rice and Stewart Patrick, *Index of State Weakness in the Developing World*, (Washington DC: Brookings Institution, 2008), p. 14.

35 Lisa Anderson, *The State and Social Transformation in Tunisia and Libya, 1830–1980* (Princeton: Princeton University Press, 1986), p. 4.

36 On the failure of Arab bureaucracies, Joseph G. Jabbra has listed the following nine reasons: newness and limitations of Arab bureaucratic structure; traditional Arab culture; concentration and diffusion of authority; lack of reliable data sets; political interference; mismatches in training and education; poor relations between bureaucracy and citizens; corruption; and staffing. See Joseph G. Jabbra, "Bureaucracy and Development in the Arab World," in Joseph G. Jabbra, ed., *Bureaucracy and Development in the Arab World* (Leiden: E.J. Brill, 1989), pp. 3–5.

37 Nazih Ayubi, "Arab Bureaucracies: Expanding Size, Changing Roles," in Adeed Dawisha and I. William Zartman, *Beyond Coercion: The Durability of the Arab State* (London: Croom Helm, 1988), pp. 24–26.

38 Paraphrasing Jamil E. Jreisat, *Politics without Process: Administrative Development in the Arab World* (Boulder: Lynne Rienner Publishers, 1997), pp. 58–61.

DOI: 10.1057/9781137504081.0005

39   *Ibid.*, p. 60.

40   Gamal Abul Hassan, "On the fighter who took his military uniform off," *Al-Masry Al-Youm*, June 22, 2014, http://m.almasryalyoum.com/news/details/468950.

41   Ibrahim Elnur, "The Implosion of Political Patronage Regimes in the Middle East," in *Egypt's Tahrir Revolution*, ed., Dan Tschirgi, Walid Kazziha, and Sean F. McMahon (Boulder: Lynne Rienner Publishers, 2013): p. 133.

42   Fukuyama, "The Imperative of State-Building," pp. 21–22.

43   Max Weber, *Theory of Social and Economic Organization* (New York: Free Press, 1964), p. 154.

44   James E. Rauch and Peter B. Evans, "Bureaucratic Structure and Bureaucratic Performance in Less Developed Countries," *Journal of Public Economics* 75, no. 1 (January 2000): pp. 49–71.

45   John G. Merriam, "Bureaucrats as Agents of Development in the Middle East," in Ali Farazmand, ed., *Handbook of Comparative and Development Public Administration* (New York: Marcel Dekker Inc., 2001): pp. 565–579.

46   *Arab Human Development Report 2002*, http://www.arab-hdr.org/publications/other/ahdr/ahdr2002e.pdf. Note that all the above-average indicators, however, are less than one standard deviation above the mean.

47   Rice and Patrick, *Index of State Weakness*, p. 20.

48   Marshall *et al.* include measures of both institutional democracy and institutional autocracy: competitiveness of the selection process of a state's chief executive, the openness of this process, the extent to which there are institutional constraints on a chief executive's decision-making authority, the competitiveness of political participation within a state, and the regulations governing this participation. These measures are combined to create additive eleven-point scales (0–10) of each state's democratic characteristics (DEMOC) and autocratic characteristics (AUTOC). The regime type value (POLITY) is derived by subtracting the AUTOC value from the DEMOC value (*DEMOC - AUTOC = POLITY*). POLITY value ranges from –10 (strongly autocratic) to +10 (strongly democratic). Composite POLITY values in 2009–2010 of the four states are as follows: Egypt (–3), Tunisia (–4), Libya (–7) and Syria (–7).

49   Khaled Fahmy, *All the Pasha's Men: Mehmed Ali, His Army and the Making of Modern Egypt* (Cairo: Dar El-Shorouk, 2014).

50   Migdal, *Strong Societies and Weak States*, p. 274.

51   Seth D. Kaplan, *Fixing Fragile States: A New Paradigm for Development* (Westport: Praeger Security International, 2008), 102.

52   Volker Perthes, "Syria under Bashar al-Assad: Modernization and the Limits of Change," *Adelphi Paper* 366 (July 2004), pp. 23–24.

53   Kaplan, *Fixing Fragile States*, pp. 102, 104.

54   Jreisat, *Politics without Process*, p. 80.

DOI: 10.1057/9781137504081.0005

55　*Economist,* http://www.economist.com/node/21606286/print.

56　Anderson, *The State and Social Transformation in Tunisia and Libya,* p. 187.

57　Lisa Anderson, "Tribe and State: Libyan Anomalies," in Philip S. Khoury and Joseph Kostiner, *Tribes and State Formation in the Middle East* (London: I.B. Tauris & Co Ltd. Publishers, 1990), p. 294.

58　Anderson, *The State and Social Transformation in Tunisia and Libya,* p. 274.

59　*Ibid.,* p. 268.

60　Wolfram Lacher, "Families, Tribes and Cities in the Libya Revolution," *Middle East Policy* XVIII, no. 4 (Winter 2011): p. 146.

61　Anderson, *The State and Social Transformation in Tunisia and Libya,* p. 274.

62　Lacher, "Families, Tribes and Cities in the Libya Revolution," p. 142.

63　*Ibid.,* p. 141.

64　Anderson, *The State and Social Transformation in Tunisia and Libya,* p. 156.

65　Daniel Zisenwine, "The Revolution's Aftermath: Tunisia's Road to a Renewed Polity," in Friedman and Maddy-Weitzman, *Inglorious Revolutions,* pp. 232–233.

66　Joseph G. Jabbra, "Bureaucracy and Development in the Arab World," p.10.

67　Mohamed Dayfi, "The administrative division became a reference to the citizen," *El-Chaab,* September 10, 2011, http://www.echaab.info.tn/detailarticle.asp?IDX=15248.

68　*Middle East Online,* "Wave of Discontent," February 20, 2015, http://middle-east-online.com/?id=193817.

DOI: 10.1057/9781137504081.0005

2
Inward-Directed Security

Abstract: *This chapter addresses the emerging inward-directed threats (e.g., political, economic and social development, creating civil society, internal security and insurgencies) that have followed the 2011 Arab Spring revolutions against authoritarian regimes. The focus of security here is essentially non-state centered, emphasizing the primarily individual connotation of the term. The argument is that the fall of security services during the Arab revolutions implied the fall of regimes, as well as the fall of state authority. This was a result not only of that it was state security atrocities that triggered the popular uprising, but also of the fact that Arab authoritarian states employed the same tool – the fear of security services – for both preventing political change and maintaining social order. This chapter examines how the post-revolutions governments have tackled these issues in a way that only intensifies the ongoing turmoil.*

Yossef, Amr and Joseph R. Cerami. *The Arab Spring and the Geopolitics of the Middle East: Emerging Security Threats and Revolutionary Change.* Basingstoke: Palgrave Macmillan, 2015. DOI: 10.1057/9781137504081.0006.

2.1   Critical security studies and the Arab Spring

The failure of international relations realists to foresee the peaceful disintegration of the Soviet Union and the end of the Cold War has given rise to the need to concentrate not only on state/system interactions but also on occurrences and variables within the state, a concentration that developed to be Critical Security Studies (CSS).[1] Similarly, it was not until the failure of Middle East specialists to foresee the collapse of Arab authoritarian regimes in 2011, particularly for the over-estimation of the stability of the military-security complex and state control over the economy,[2] that more focused attention of the Arab world's security within CSS was raised.

Though the Arab world has never been excluded from the CSS explanations even before the Arab Spring revolutions in 2011, the limited literature in this regard remained inadequate. For example, Mohammed Ayoob did identify some Arab states, such as Somalia, as part of the Third World whose internal security problems emanated from the incomplete state building – translated into quasi states and failed states – and aspirations to ethnic self-determination.[3] However, Ayoob's account appears to having been influenced by the former Yugoslavia disintegration experience, especially the ethnic dimension, that he overlooked particular attributes that characterize the Arab world's reality. Similarly, Bahgat Korany *et al.* opened the 1993 edited volume, *The Many Faces of National Security in the Arab World*, with strong criticism of the conventional realist national security paradigm with its emphasis on geopolitics and military threats, though it ends up discussing mainly these same topics of military security of territorial states at the regional level.[4]

In her 2005 *Regional Security in the Middle East: A Critical Perspective*, Pinar Bilgin presented a more focused attempt, criticizing the[5] spatial representations of the Middle East – "Middle East", "Arab Regional System", "Euro-Med Region" and "Muslim Middle East" – each of which excludes the others' concerns and falls short of addressing peoples' genuine security needs. Nevertheless, Bilgin's account fell short of "broadening security" as it paid little attention to the very issues she has identified as endangering security in the Middle East, such as human-rights abuses, illiteracy, militarization of society, and environmental degradation.

DOI: 10.1057/9781137504081.0006

Most of the post-Arab Spring CSS literature has focused more on the occurrences in pre- and during the revolution time and less on those that have been taking place in the post-revolution time.[6] Alternatively, much ink has been spilled over exploring the potential non-military security implications of the Arab Spring for the Mediterranean region in an exclusively outward-directed approach.[7] Therefore, little attention has been paid to applying CSS in a way that would address non-military security threats for outward- and inward-directed referents alike, a lacuna that this chapter attempts to bridge.

As a constitutive theory, CSS has three main goals: (1) deepening security, to connect the concept of security with the deeper assumptions about the nature of politics, so that a deepened concept of security would provide an emancipatory alternative in terms of alternative institutions and practices; (2) broadening security, to tackle security issues beyond the traditional concern with military threats; and (3) extending security, to shift the "reference object" of security discourse in a way in which individual humans – and not states – are the ultimate referent of security.[8] Corresponding to these three goals, we would analyze the events in Egypt, Syria, Tunisia and Libya to demonstrate that the collapse of authoritarian regimes created an "authority vacuum" that resulted in two major security threats for these countries' individual citizens – as the referents of security – which are insecurity from violence and insecurity from want. These insecurities, in turn, have helped create the largest human security concern for the Mediterranean since the civil war in former Yugoslavia in 1991, manifested in the waves of illegal immigration and refugees arriving in the EU countries.

The focus of security here is essentially non-state centered, emphasizing the primarily individual connotation of the term. However, this emphasis on the primacy of the individual does not mean that security of the individual can be divorced from other realms of human and social concerns when it comes to dealing with security issues. In other words, when developments in other realms – ranging from the economic to the political – threaten to have immediate consequences for the individual's sense of security, these other variables shall be taken into account as part of an individual's security calculations. That is to say those economic, social, cultural, and ecological concerns do not become part of the individual's security for our purposes unless they threaten to have outcomes that directly affect the individual citizens' sense of security in their daily lives.

DOI: 10.1057/9781137504081.0006

2.2   The double fall of regime and public order

In 2004, Syrian opposition leader Burhan Ghaliounin argued that "despotism provokes anarchy by systematically destroying all the political, civil, ethical, and moral bonds that ensure the endurance and stability of society,"[9] and therefore Arab regimes benefited from the compliance of the West that wanted to guard against the risk that worse, extremist regimes might arise. The implications of this argument proved even wider in the period that followed the success of the Arab Spring revolutions.

The fall of security services during the Arab revolutions implied the fall of regimes, as well as the fall of state authority. This was a result not only of that it was state security atrocities that triggered the popular uprising, thanks to their infamous practices against their own citizens, including arbitrary arrests and torture, but also of the fact that Arab authoritarian states employed the same tool – the fear of security services – for both preventing political change and maintaining social order.

First and foremost, the mere fact that Arab authoritarian regimes have been able to remain in power for decades despite the availability of several considerations of their overthrow, revolving around the weakness or failure of their respective states, has traditionally been explained by scholars almost exclusively by the successful coercion and oppression the Arab security services employed. In 1988, explaining the durability of the Arab state, Adeed Dawisha and William Zartman cautioned not to underestimate "the effectiveness of internal security apparatuses in the Arab state, both as an instrument to control potential opposition, and as a means of combating such opposition in the event control fails."[10] Sixteen years later, in 2004, Eva Bellin similarly attributed the Arab state's enduring authoritarianism "to the robustness of the coercive apparatus in many Middle Eastern and North African states and to this apparatus's exceptional will and capacity to crush democratic initiatives."[11]

Second, the role the security apparatus played in maintaining the stability of the Arab authoritarian regimes was only the top of the iceberg. In each Arab state, security services rather constituted a "securitocracy" that is a system of security elites that use their direct and indirect influence in matters that range from strict security policy to foreign policy to finance and economic policies.[12] In the shadow of a failed bureaucracy and a culture of fear, Arab security services had a say

DOI: 10.1057/9781137504081.0006

in almost anything going on in the state. In the words of Saad El-Din Ibrahim:

> The security apparatus has been, and still, a main tool in imposing the hegemony of the state and the ruling regime ... Arab Ministries of Interior, whose responsibility is maintaining security, are among the largest in size, resources and influence. In some [Arab] states, the Ministry of Interior assumes some responsibilities that are uncharacteristic to the nature of this Ministry in most non-Arab states. Sometimes, it assumes, in addition to the direct responsibility of maintaining security, the responsibilities of supervising over education, health care, municipalities, volunteer organization, prisons and elections. Once the short liberal moment, witnessed by some Arab states soon after their independence, was over, the security establishment (the Ministry of Interior) turned into the real top of the executive authority.[13]

The overstating of the Arab securitocracy, that is the widespread intervention of the security apparatuses in the businesses of the other ministries and state agencies, had a double effect on the Arab state. Drawing on Guillermo O'Donnell's levels of political accountability,[14] this intervention influenced the state vertically (power relations between the state and its citizens, in an over-dependence on the security apparatuses in the management of the state affairs within a culture of fear from the state – *haybat al-dawla*), and horizontally (absent checks-and-balances within the state, institutional oversight by securitocracy over other ministries and state agencies further weakened the already-weak state bureaucracy, since interventions by securitocracy are status-quo oriented and hardly based on relevant professional grounds).

Unfortunately, the testimony to the success of securitocracy has been the durability of the authoritarian leaderships on the top of Arab weak or failed states for decades. Nevertheless, this securitocracy was designed and operated essentially to prevent the overthrow of the ruling leadership by an organized group (such as Islamists), and particularly the seizure of the state by an organized group within the state apparatus, i.e., coup-proofing.[15] It was precisely for this reason that this securitocracy failed to prevent, and later to suppress, the Arab Spring protests, characterized not by traditional revolutionary tactics, that is a small, ideological and organized group that gradually attracts the sympathy of the masses leading to mass revolt, but rather by leaderless demonstrations, spontaneously assembled through social media websites, involving tens of thousands of angry people, especially the young, demanding an end to the rule of the regime in power, that simply overwhelmed the

DOI: 10.1057/9781137504081.0006

capacity of the regular police and intelligence services. Consequently, in the words of Bellin, "in every Arab country where serious protest erupted, regime survival ultimately turned on one question: would the military defect? Or, more specifically, would the military shoot the protesters or not?".[16]

Notably, as it has been the case with explaining the Arab Spring revolutions as well as the relative success or failure of their transitional processes, scholars have conventionally adopted the view that the decision to shoot or not depended in large part on the homogenous nature of the particular military's society, whereas in homogenous societies (such as Egypt and Tunisia), the militaries chose not to shoot, while in less-homogenous societies where the military serves as the instrument of the ruler's family or tribe (such as in Libya and Syria), the militaries chose to shoot.[17] Little attention has been paid, however, to the potential that it was the stateness variable in each of the four countries, in terms of the ability and professionalism of the state bureaucracy, in which the military constitutes an important part especially in post-colonial states such as those in the Middle East, which corresponds to the different positions of the militaries towards defending the regime in power.

In the final analysis, the effect of this double fall, regime and public order, was immediately reflected in the state of lawlessness and economic crisis ensuring the start of each pro-democracy revolution. In the Arab Spring countries, the defeat of the security apparatuses, responsible for the regime security as well as decades-long human rights violations, cannot be exaggerated. Nevertheless, the impact of this defeat was larger than its parts. Well beyond falling the regimes in Tunisia, Egypt and Libya and shaking the regime in Syria, the defeat of the security apparatuses immediately led to the fall of *haybat al-dawla* vertically, that is citizens – providers and recipients of state public services alike – were no longer committed to the same law-binding behavior they were previously used to. By and large, this has been a situation in which not only the citizens behaved unconstrained by the rule of law but also, and more importantly, the control over the state institutions, long practiced by the securitocracy, was loosening, especially at a time when this very same securitocracy has traditionally been the most able among the state bureaucracy.

Interestingly, though sadly, this has not only confirmed the double meaning of the Arabic word "*nezam*" – "regime" and "public order" – but also materialized the old Egyptian regime's "Mubarak-or-chaos" dualism,

DOI: 10.1057/9781137504081.0006

echoing Iraq in 2003 when the sudden lift of a suppressive government unleashed violence and lawlessness.[18]

2.3   Insecurity from violence, insecurity from want

The fall of the security apparatus not only resulted in the natural outcome of deteriorating security, with all that might entail for economic development projects and investment, but also weakened the already-weak state bureaucracy, resulting in another deterioration in the provision of public services. As we shall see in the next pages, the post-revolutions governments in Egypt, Tunisia and Libya and the several "governing bodies" in Syria, have equally failed to tackle these problems and offer a significant improvement in the lives of their citizens. Instead, they have, by and large, tackled these problems in a way that only intensified the on-going turmoil. The obstacles to presenting serious solutions to these problems are very close to the obstacles to reforming the security sector in the Arab world, as described in 2013 by Omar Ashour, especially the following: the extreme political polarization that leads to politicization of reform and political violence, internal resistance to reform by the anti-reform elements; and limited government capacity and limited knowledge and experience among those who are supposed to implement reform.[19] It appears that post-revolution governments have, unlike their populations, focused more on the "who governs?" and not the "how well?" question.

Though many scholars agree that domestic violence is historically inseparable from revolutions, along the experience of the French, Russian, and Iranian revolutions,[20] what distinguishes the continuing violence in Arab Spring countries, with the exception of Syria, is that it was not the result of the struggle between forces of the new regime and those of the old regime. Rather, this violence is mainly the result of the lawlessness that ensured the increasing inability of government to provide security.

In what Adeel Malik and Bassem Awadallah call "the original sin" of the Arab world economy – that is the reliance on unearned income, either oil revenues or foreign aid – the state was the provider of basic public goods, such as food, energy, and jobs, in a system that persisted through a combination of repression and redistribution.[21] In the aftermath of the Arab Spring, however, the fall of the old regimes resulted in the

DOI: 10.1057/9781137504081.0006

fall of the two apparently mutually-dependent pillars of this economic model: repression and redistribution. In other words, the failure of the post-revolution governments to provide security and rule of law in their sovereign territories has created a situation in which these governments are neither capable of providing a safe environment for domestic and foreign investments nor of receiving the revenues required to satisfy the increasing demands of populations that are no longer sensitive to the old formula of repression. Below is a general survey of the post-revolution deteriorating economic situation, or insecurity from want, in the four Arab Spring countries before we move to a more detailed discussion of each country.

The economic impact of the fall of "public order" was grave. In the words of Erik Berglof and Shanta Devarajan: "Political assassinations and polarization in Tunisia, civil unrest and a military takeover in Egypt, terrorist attacks in Yemen, sectarian strife and an institutional vacuum in Libya, and civil war in Syria have contributed to a sharp fall in investment, tourism, exports, and GDP growth, aggravating macroeconomic imbalances."[22] Hong Kong and Shanghai Banking Corporation (HSBC) estimates that the cost of the Arab Spring for the seven most affected countries would be $800 billion by the end of 2014.[23] In a region where governments remain dependent on oil revenues, the continuing fall of public order had forced foreign investors to refrain from further investing in this area. As one analyst put it "The prospects for the oil and gas sector in countries like Libya are nonexistent for the next few years.... The main problem is that many of these governments are just not in control on the ground."[24]

Foreign aid has indeed been offered. The European Union has committed itself in May 2011 to provide €1.24 billion to the Middle East and North Africa region (MENA) countries; and at the Deauville summit, the G-8 group decided that to provide $20 billion for Tunisia and Egypt through the international development banks, primarily the European Investment Bank and the European Bank for Reconstruction and Development. However, thus far neither much of these European funds, nor the $2.5 billion promised by the United States, have been received by these two countries. Also, the Gulf countries have contributed roughly $28 billion to transition countries, but these funds were mainly used to cover budget deficits and finance subsidies and wages, rather than in public investment projects that would help a sustainable economic growth. Even if foreign aid continues at the present rate, it would not

DOI: 10.1057/9781137504081.0006

likely suffice to satisfy the needs for long-term economic reforms, esti-mated at $30-40 billion annually for about three years.[25]

At the same time, structural reforms in the Arab Spring countries, such as cutting subsidies that the European Bank for Reconstruction and Development recommends,[26] does not appear to be an easy option for governments that are not able to contain public backlash. For example, in March 2013, when Egyptian bakers started a strike against the insuf-ficient bread subsidies, economists warned against "revolution of the hungry," and the government had eventually to back down, at the expense of increasing public debt.[27] In particular, according to the International Monetary Fund and the World Bank studies, current account deficit of 2013 in most Arab Spring countries is estimated to be 6% of GDP, which equals, in three years, its value in any previous ten years, which approaches 70% of these countries GDPs.[28]

The end result of this vicious circle – slow economic growth breeds social unrest which, in turn, delays economic recovery – is insecurity from want. According to the International Labor Organization estimates, due to the ongoing social unrest, unemployment rates in the MENA region – where 25% of the active workforce unemployed – have increased between 3.5% to 7%. Youth employment rate is the highest in the world, ranging between 27% to 29%, which is almost double the global average. The ILO report notes that even educational attainment does not help a lot as statistics show that unemployment among college graduates in the Arab Spring countries is estimated at 40%.[29]

2.3.1   Egypt

The US Department of State's Overseas Security Advisory Council (OSAC) Crime and Safety report portrays a bad picture of the average citizens' insecurity from violence. Though of increasing rates from January 2011 to March 2014, crime appeared to be decreasing afterwards as the visibility of police has increased, and crime has generally leveled off, though cases of carjackings and kidnappings are reported much more frequently than before.[30] Notwithstanding the type of violence – political, crime, or sectarian – the insecurity from violence resulted from either from the excess in using forces (such as the November/December 2011 confrontations with protesters in Cairo) or shortage in using force (such as the reluctance of the police to intervene in the Port Said stadium violence which led to 79 deaths in February 2012) to enforce law and maintain order. The rise in crime rates, police failure and inflow of weapons from across the borders, especially in Libya, all combined to encourage citizens' willingness to take law into their own hands.[31]

The cause for Egyptian police's failure to restore order is multifaceted, but still centered around the fact that it was this same police that the Mubarak regime used to oppress opposition and unrest before and during the revolution. One facet of this failure is the demoralization of the police force – which appeared as a "broken army" after its "defeat" at the hand of protestors who, during the 18 days of uprising, torched more than 95 police stations and 4000 vehicles[32] – to the extent that police personnel were not able to appear in their uniform in public for some time after the revolution. Citizens facing crime-in-action frequently receive negligent replies from the police. Another facet is the unwillingness or inability to adapt to the changing environment – "confronted by a population that may no longer fear retribution or respect their authority or ability to adequately enforce the law."[33] As a major in the Egyptian Central Security Forces (the riot police) testified on the confrontations with protestors in the post-revolution time: "The pattern we have here is that the officer gets attacked with shotguns and Molotov cocktails. If he flees, he gets accused of negligence, and then he goes to trial. If he fights back, he gets accused of brutality, and then he gets tried as well. What exactly is he supposed to do?"[34]

Deterioration in security led to deterioration in economic conditions, particularly in the tourism sector that is considered one of the main sources of income and employment in the country, providing foreign direct investment, economic growth and foreign reserves. Facing dire economic prospects, President Sisi opted for reducing the petroleum and electricity subsidies, which resulted directly in rising prices of almost all commodities and services.

No other case than Egypt can better illustrate the case of political polarization. After one year in power in which he could not re-start the economy or provide security, former President Mohamed Morsi (of the Muslim Brotherhood) was ousted in a popular revolution supported by the military. Political violence ensued, not only from MB members who continued to organize demonstrations against the new rule, but also from the affiliate Islamist organizations, primarily the Sinai-based Ansar Bayet al-Maqdes (ABM), that is conducting a campaign of terror targeting the army and police forces in the northern Sinai, resulting in the death and injury of hundreds of soldiers. It would be an underestimation, however, to ascribe the deteriorated security situation merely to the political

DOI: 10.1057/9781137504081.0006

polarization, though it is true that both parties have been investing essentially in excluding the other than to improve the services provided.

Nevertheless, the bureaucracies, including the security apparatus's, resistance to reform as well as the chronic problems of the Egyptian bureaucracy as elaborated above in Chapter 1 still constitutes the major obstacle before passing this period of security and economic deterioration.

2.3.2   Libya

The country faces bankruptcy as its oil exports, which constitute 95% of government revenues, have either stalled or being transferred outside of the government control, and total exports fell to a quarter of what it was before the revolution. According to the Libyan Ministry of Economy, the oil blockades cost the Libyan economy over $10 billion in 2013. Foreign investors fled from the country and all major infrastructure projects have been suspended and looted.[35] Unemployment is rampant and few people could rely on a stable source of income. According to the US Department of State's "Libya Travel Warning" of January 2015, crime levels remain high in many parts of Libya and authorities do not have control over much of the country throughout which ongoing clashes and attacks by armed groups frequently occur.[36]

As state institutions have all but collapsed, the country is experiencing internal chaos. Apart from the terrorist attack against the US diplomatic mission on Benghazi in September 11, 2012, the OSAC report describes a situation in which 16,000 criminals who escaped prison remained free, and carjackings, robberies, burglaries and thefts are routine. More acute is the proliferation of small arms. The fast collapse of the military and police forces loyal to the former leader Muammar Qaddafi, in addition to the international no-fly zone imposed over Libya in March 2011 and NATO tactical air support, enabled the rebels to gain access to the Qaddafi army's inventories, including enormous stock of assault rifles, light machine guns, and grenades.[37] This enormous stock of small weapons allowed the emergence of two phenomena. First, several thousands of individuals managed to keep small arms in their possession and are using these in crimes and vendettas free from law enforcement retribution. Second, the access to these arms allowed the persistence of a plethora of armed militias – even after the fall of the Qaddafi regime – who are responsible for human rights abuses, kidnappings and assassinations, let along inter-militia clashes.[38] Under the circumstances, security is a mirage. The Libyan academic Mustafa Fetouri wrote in 2015:

DOI: 10.1057/9781137504081.0006

The security situation is worse still. Parents do not know whether it is safe enough to let their children go unaccompanied to the local school. At night, one is likely to be declared missing if not home by 10 p.m. Most women do not drive any longer and stay mostly indoors for weeks on end. I still remember the times when I would rarely lock my car or my house, and women were safe to drive at night on Tripoli's main streets. Families would gather in cafes and at the seafront until late and nothing would threaten them. We, Libyans, used to take security and safety for granted. It was extremely rare to hear of an explosion or car bomb attack. Today, explosions and even suicide attacks are frequent in Tripoli.[39]

In a failed state, dubbed "The Land of Militias," public order and the economy in Libya are in complete disarray since various militias are occupying several parts of the country. The militarization of the February 17 revolution started as a result of the decision by Qaddafi to crackdown on the peaceful protesters, and therefore armed groups formed in "liberated" areas. Even after the fall of the regime, the proliferation of armed groups and militias continued for reasons ranging from vendettas, to conflicts over resources and the unprecedented spread of weapons, but essentially the decision by the interim National Transitional Council to call on citizens form local civil and military councils to maintain security and order in the country. The NTC made this call precisely because of the collapse of the military and security apparatus and the lack of control over Western Libya. This decision appears to be part of the NTC tendency to fight – absurdly, it now seems – the remnants of the Qaddafi's ancient regime and with an eye to counterbalance the emerging Islamists militia. Other faulty decisions include establishing the so-called "Higher Security Committee", formed by the Ministry of Interior that attracted a hundred thousand of unemployed youth, which has empowered this force at the expense of the official police force. A similar action was undertaken by the Ministry of Defense that established Libya's Shield Force as a support for the regular Libyan army.[40]

When the Islamists lost the first democratic elections in July 2012 (winning 17 out of 80 seats in the General National Congress), they sabotaged the functioning of three successive, short-lived governments headed by Mustafa Abu Shagour, Ali Zeidan and Abdullah al-Thani. A failed attempt to decide the conflict against the Islamists by retired general Khalifa Hifter led to another election in June 2014 of the House of Representatives. Again, the Islamists lost though with an 18% turn-out rate, and then rejected the elections result, and resided in Tripoli, that was invaded in August 2014 by Islamist militia, to convene

DOI: 10.1057/9781137504081.0006

the new General National Congress, while the House of Representatives convened in the eastern city of Tobrouk.

Qaddafi left behind neither a military, a coherent security apparatus, nor a civilian bureaucracy – a typical "authority vacuum." Therefore, when he eventually fell, nobody in Libya was powerful enough to disarm the militias. Instead, the NTC found it in its interest to fund these militias to preempt a scenario in which the old regime returns. In retrospect, the current situation ever since August 2014 as the country is divided in what can be described as a low-intensity civil war between Islamists an non-Islamists, can be traced back to political polarization or the focus of each of the two conflicting sides on the exclusion of the other, as well as the personalities of the Qaddafi regime, instead of focusing on re-establishing state authority. Equally important is the absence of adequate knowledge and competence at the bureaucratic levels in the successive governments, either in Tripoli or Tobrouk, to re-build and introduce the needed reforms in state institutions. Combined, these factors help sustain the status-quo of the state absence in Libya.

2.3.3   Tunisia

Tunisia is struggling with some very serious economic problems. A quarter of the population lives under $4 per day, and inflation is at around 6%, and the trade deficit continued to worsen. Foreign direct investment has been falling sharply. According to one report, "the basic economic framework of institutions, regulation, and corruption hasn't changed and is still concentrating wealth while preventing growth in employment."[41] Unemployment in Tunisia though slightly down than the last two years, is at 15.2% and it is the highest among any of its neighbors. Among the youth, the situation is even worse as youth employment is over 30%.[42]

Deteriorating economic conditions were accompanied by a similar deterioration in the security situation, especially on the borders with Algeria and Libya. As is the case in Egypt and Libya, the OSAC report notes the increased rate of criminal activity with the existence of a significant rate of violent and non-violent crimes that go in tandem with availability of small arms and other weapons in the country and the police excessive use of force against protesters in sit-ins and strikes resulting in several deaths and injuries.[43]

Political polarization in Tunisia has been mitigated, through the Al-Nahda party's (Tunisia's Muslim Brotherhood) agreement to share power with the National Salvation Front (Tunisia's union of secular parties) in an interim government in 2013 and the endorsement of the new constitution in February 2014, and then holding, most recently, new parliamentary elections in October 2014 and then presidential elections in November in which the centrist party "Nidaa Tunis" (a part of National Salvation Front) won the majority and the presidential office.

Nevertheless, the government is facing a rising security threat from the Ansar Al-Shari'a organization that had successfully targeted the police and military on several occasions, especially in the Mount Chaambi region. Most recently, in March 2015, an attack by terrorists at the renowned Bardo Museum in central Tunis left 24 people dead and 47 injured. In essence, the country had been facing, much like Egypt, a police failure, thanks to both demoralization and unwillingness/inability to adapt to a changing environment.

One example is the trial of Colonel Moncef al-Ajimi, the former director of the Tunisian Intervention Forces, who was accused of firing on peaceful protestors during the revolution. In reaction, "hundreds of policemen from the Bouchoucha barracks physically blocked access to al-Ajimi and then organized a strike to protest his attempted dismissal. Thousands of Intervention Forces members withdrew from key locations in several Tunisian cities and returned to their barracks."[44] Another example is the police failure to investigate the several cases of physical assaults on intellectuals, human rights activists, and journalists carried out by extremists, most likely belonging to the Ansar al-Sharia group. Most notable is the assassinations of Chokri Belaid, an outspoken opponent of the al-Nahda party in February 2013 and opposition leader Mohamed Brahmi in July 2013.

Regardless of the professionalism of the police, the Tunisia is yet to extend its full "stateness" to the south of the country, particularly on the borders with Algeria and Libya. There is scant wonder, therefore, that it is these impoverished provinces, that constitute almost half of the country, that supply recruits to the terrorist organizations operating either in Tunisia or abroad in Libya, Syria and Iraq.[45]

2.3.4 Syria

It is hard to exaggerate the horrifying insecurity situation as a result of the ongoing conflict there following the popular revolution against the Bashar al-Assad regime. Both the government and the opposition forces have committed massive human rights violations in the

DOI: 10.1057/9781137504081.0006

conflict that, as of August 2014, according to the United Nations High Commission for Human Rights, has claimed more than 191,000 lives and displaced several millions.[46] The spread and intensification of war have led to a huge humanitarian crisis. The United Nations High Commissioner for Refugees has estimated that, by mid-2014, 10.8 million of Syria's 22 million population will be affected and in need of humanitarian assistance, including 6.5 million internally displaced, often multiple times, which could probably constitute the world's largest refugee population.[47]

Less media attention, however, has been given to the criminal violence and lawlessness thriving in Syrian cities in which the controlling authority – either the government or the rebels – maintain little effort for the protection of citizens. The tragedy of the combination of economic misery, unemployment and absence of security has produced an expansion of a "makework" activity within the economy, with an increasing share of Syrian youth joining the recruitment of combatants in the various fighting factions, but also, and more importantly for the security of the average non-combatant Syrians, join various criminal networks engaging in conflict-related enterprises and illegal activities, including human trafficking and abuse, pillage, smuggling, kidnapping and extortion.[48] One citizen of Aleppo once summarized the situation as such: "Chaos, lawlessness, fear, it is just so chaotic, and with all the thugs in the streets, you never know who might kidnap you and ask for a ransom."[49]

Even much less attention has been paid to the worsening economic situation of those who continue to live inside Syria. According to one report, life expectancy has fallen from 75.9 years to 55.7 years, 80% are in poverty and 30% in "abject poverty", 51% of children no longer attend school and economic losses are more than $202 billion – 383% of the GDP of 2010 whereas the budget deficit increased from 35.7% in 2013 to 40.5% in 2014. Unemployment has risen from 14.9% in 2011 to 57.7% by the end of 2014. The total number of unemployed is 3.72 million people, of whom 2.96 million lost their jobs during the conflict, losing income impacting on the welfare of 12.22 million dependents. Combined, these factors led the Human Development Index value of Syria to fall by 32.6%, moving the country from a mid-ranking position to 173 of 187 countries.[50]

Considering the Syrian revolution as a part of international conspiracy against Syria, Assad has rejected any negotiations on a transition of power, leaving millions of Syrians to suffer under his government whose performance got only worse during the conflict. In a strong reminder both

DOI: 10.1057/9781137504081.0006

of the weakness of the Syrian state as the source of the revolution and its consequences, Louay Hussein wrote under the title "The Syrians do not feel the need to the state," that since the Syrian regime has destroyed the social structures of the state, tribe and sect, the Syrian individual has not had in this conflict any structure to involve in but the regional one, and therefore welcomed "any group that could provide him some protection and some services, even if this was a fundamental group."[51]

The so-called the Islamic State (IS) organization represents the extremist form of Islamist ideology and legitimization as it has declared, in June 2014, the re-establishment of the caliphate to rule over all Muslims, and has taken foot where the state has collapsed in Syria and Iraq. Nevertheless, it soon started to show its own "weakness" as manifested in the failure to govern a model Islamic state. The increasing inability to deliver services is to the detriment of several millions living under its rule of Sunni populations who initially welcomed IS precisely for the failure of their respective states in Syria and Iraq.[52] Perhaps the only good news is the experience of the rebel groups in control of Aleppo, Idlib and East Ghouta, in the Damascus province. Administrative bodies were created and run by local actors for the provision of basic services. In the words of Ilina Angelova, "This civilian administration model, similar to the one implemented in the "liberated" areas ... is considered by many civilians and members of the opposition as an embodiment of the original principles of the Syrian revolution."[53]

2.4   An exodus to Europe?

Economic crisis and absence of security is best illustrated in the exodus of illegal migrants from North Africa to the European Union through the Mediterranean. True, the Arab Spring has not created the illegal migration which existed years before, but it did certainly exacerbate it in two ways. First, the pool of willing migrants had sharply increased thanks to the dire economic and security situation in their countries of origin. Waves of boats carrying illegal migrants departing mainly from Libya, Tunisia and Egypt (but also from Algeria and Morocco), brought about 141,000 people to Europe through the Mediterranean Sea only in 2014.

Following the 2013 Lampedusa migrant shipwreck, the Italian Navy started Operation Mare Nostrum to intercept ships carrying migrants in international waters, an operation that intercepted more than 140,000

DOI: 10.1057/9781137504081.0006

people up until October 2014 when it was replaced by operation Triton, run by the EU's border agency, Frontex. Following the feared death of 950 people in an immigrant shipwreck in the Mediterranean in April 2015, European leaders agreed on four priority areas for action: "to strengthen the EU's presence at sea, to fight the traffickers, to prevent illegal migration flows and to reinforce internal solidarity and responsibility", with a focus on re-establishing government authority in Libya.[54]

Nevertheless, the summit made it clear that the EU does not have a decisive a successful solution to this problem, especially when it considering that operations *a la* Mare Nostrum, that is in essence saving the immigrants, could turn into a way of attraction rather than deterrence of the wave of illegal immigrants, especially at a time when there are estimates that, as of April 2015, a huge number of people, ranging between 500,000 to one million people are waiting on the Libyan shores to cross the Mediterranean to Europe. In short, the continuation of the economic crisis and the absence of security had already led to a drastic increase in the number of refugees, especially from Syria, and are also likely to generate greater waves of illegal migration if no serious improvements are taking place. At the same time, almost certainly there will be an accumulative effect of these migration waves on Europe which is already suffering under an economic crisis, which could easily play into the hands of the extreme right-wing parties. If added to terrorism threats coming from the Mediterranean too, this could lead to a wave of hatred and the rejection of the immigrant communities in Europe, especially the Muslim communities.

Second, the ability of security forces in the south Mediterranean countries, especially Libya, to fight illegal immigration has significantly decreased thanks to the ongoing turmoil in these countries. In the pre-revolution time, it was possible to depend on the governments there to enforce the law and even reach workable agreements on that basis. For example, in 2008, Italy and Libya began joint naval patrols to stop boatloads of illegal immigrants from crossing the Mediterranean. Also, in 2010, Libya signed a €50 billion deal with the European Union to manage its borders as a "transit country" for sub-Saharan Africans. The situation is currently different where the Libyan security forces, lacking both experience and resources, are simply unable to stop the waves of illegal immigrants, either in the south, where sub-Saharan Africans cross the border to Libya, or in the north, where illegal migrants leave their "transit country" to their final destination in Europe.[55] These issues of human security are also being addressed more frequently by US policymakers – in

DOI: 10.1057/9781137504081.0006

reflecting on the needs for new security approaches – in the aftermath of the initial military success in the wars in Iraq and Afghanistan, as we show in Chapter 4.

Notes

1   Richard Wyn Jones, *Security, Strategy and Critical Theory* (Boulder: Lynne Reinner Publishers, 1999), pp. 96–97.
2   F. Gregory Gause III, "Why Middle East Studies Missed the Arab Spring," *Foreign Affairs* 90, no. 4 (July/August 2011): pp 81–90.
3   Mohammed Ayoob, *The Third World Security Predicament: State Making, Regional Conflict, and the International System* (Boulder: Lynne Rienner Publishers, 1995), pp. 165–188.
4   Bahgat Korany, Paul Noble and Rex Brynen, ed., *The Many Faces of National Security in the Arab World* (London: Palgrave Macmillan, 1993).
5   Pinar Bilgin, *Regional Security in the Middle East: A Critical Perspective* (New York: Routledge, 2005).
6   See, for example, Mohammed Nuruzzaman, "Human Security and the Arab Spring," *Strategic Analysis* 37, no. 1 (January–February 2013): 52–64; Johansson-Nogués Elisabeth, "Gendering the Arab Spring? Rights and (in) security of Tunisian, Egyptian and Libyan women," *Security Dialogue* 44, no. 5–6 (October 2013): 393–409; Paul Amar, "Turning the Gendered Politics of the Security State Inside Out?" International *Feminist Journal of Politics* 13, no. 3 (September 2011): pp. 299–328.
7   See, for example, Rym Ayadi and Carlo Sessa, "What scenarios for the Euro-Mediterranean in 2030 in the wake of the post-Arab spring?," *MEDPRO Policy Paper* No. 2 (October 2011); Shimon Stein, "The European Union and the Arab Spring," in Yoel Guzansky and Mark A. Heller, ed., *One Year of the Arab Spring: Global and Regional Implications* (Tel Aviv: The Institute for National Security Studies, 2012): 25–28; Giuseppe Campesi, "The Arab Spring and the Crisis of European Border Regime: Manufacturing Emergency in the Lampedusa Crisis," EUI Working Papers RSCAS 2011/59 (Badia Feisolana: European University Institute, 2011); Anthony Cordesman, "Rethinking the Arab 'Spring': Stability and Security in Egypt, Libya Tunisia, and the Rest of the MENA Region" (Washington D.C.: Center for Strategic & International Studies, 2011).
8   Ken Booth, "Security and Emancipation," *Review of International Studies* 17, no. 4 (October 1991): 313–326; Jones, *Security, Strategy and Critical Theory*, pp. 102–112.
9   Burhan Ghalioun, "The Persistence of Arab Authoritarianism," *Journal of Democracy* 15, no. 4 (October 2004): p. 131.
10 Dawisha and Zartman, *Beyond Coercion*, p. 276.

DOI: 10.1057/9781137504081.0006

11   Eva Bellin, "The Robustness of Authoritarianism in the Middle East: Exceptionalism in Comparative Perspective," *Comparative Politics* 36, no. 2 (January 2004): pp. 139–157.

12   Juha P. Mäkelä, "The Arab Spring's Impact on Egypt Securitocracy," *International Journal of Intelligence and CounterIntelligence* 27, no. 2 (March 2014): p. 218.

13   Ibrahim, *Mustaqbal al-mujtama' wa al-dawla fi al-watan al-Arabi*, pp. 180–181.

14   Guillermo O'Donnell, "Horizontal Accountability in New Democracies," in Andreas Schedler, Larry Diamond and Marc F. Plattner, eds., *The Self-Restraining State: Power and Accountability in New Democracies* (Boulder: Lynne Reinner, 1999).

15   James T. Quinlivan, "Coup-Proofing: Its Practice and Consequences in the Middle East," *International Security* 24, no. 2 (Autumn 1999): pp. 131–165.

16   Eva Bellin, "Reconsidering the Robustness of Authoritarianism in the Middle East: Lessons from the Arab Spring," *Comparative Politics* 44, no. 2 (January 2012): 130.

17   See, for example, F. Gregory Gause III, "Why Middle East Studies Missed the Arab Spring," and Philippe Droz-Vincent, "Prospects for 'Democratic Control of the Armed Forces'?: Comparative Insights and Lessons for the Arab World in Transition," *Armed Forces & Society* 40, no. 4 (October 2014): pp. 701–702.

18   Ironically, during the Egyptian revolution, pro-regime slogans included "Yes to Mubarak; Egypt will not be another Iraq."

19   Omar Ashour, "Finishing the Job: Security Sector Reform After the Arab Spring," *World Politics Review*, May 28, 2013, http://www.brookings.edu/research/articles/2013/05/28-security-sector-reform-mena-ashour.

20   Vanessa A. Arslanian, "Beyond Revolution: Ending Lawlessness and Impunity During Revolutionary Periods," *Boston College International and Comparative Law Review* 36, no. 1 (2013): 129–133.

21   Adeel Malik and Bassem Awadallah, "The Economics of the Arab Spring," *World Development* 45 (May 2013):pp. 261–262.

22   Erik Berglof and Shanta Devarajan, "The Arab Awakening's Aftermath," *Project Syndicate*, October 10, 2013, http://www.project-syndicate.org/commentary/erik-berglof-and-shanta-devarajanon-the-arab-spring-countries--economic-prospects.

23   Peter Guest, "No fiscal space for Arab Spring countries," *Emerging Markets*, October 10, 2013, http://www.emergingmarkets.org/Article/3265631/No-fiscal-space-for-Arab-Spring-countries.html.

24   Mark Scott, "As Stability Eludes Region, Western Oil Giants Hesitate," *New York Times*, October 1, 2013, http://www.nytimes.com/2013/10/02/business/energy-environment/as-stability-eludes-region-western-oil-giants-hesitate.html.

25   Berglof and Devarajan, "The Arab Awakening's Aftermath."

26   Antonia Oprita, "EBRD to Arab Spring countries: cut subsidies," *Emerging Markets*, October 9, 2013, http://www.emergingmarkets.org/Article/3265118/EBRD-to-Arab-Spring-countries-cut-subsidies.html.

DOI: 10.1057/9781137504081.0006

27 Patrick Kingsley, "Bakers become latest victims of Egypt subsidy cuts," *The Guardian*, March 19, 2013, http://www.theguardian.com/world/2013/mar/19/bakers-egyptian-subsidy-cuts.

28 Kamal Fayad, "Arab Spring countries witness slow economic growth," *Al-Monitor*, Feb. 28, 2014, http://www.al-monitor.com/pulse/business/2014/02/arab-spring-countries-slow-economic-growth.html#ixzz2uz9kjicH.

29 *International Labor Organization*, "Global Employment Trends 2014: Risk of a Jobless Recovery," http://www.ilo.org/wcmsp5/groups/public/---dgreports/---dcomm/---publ/documents/publication/wcms_233953.pdf.

30 U.S. Department of State, "Egypt 2015 OSAC Crime and Safety Report," https://www.osac.gov/pages/ContentReportDetails.aspx?cid=17373.

31 Gamal Abu el-Hassan, "How much does the head of Taha Hussein weigh?" *Almasry Alyoum*, March 4, 2013, http://www.almasryalyoum.com/news/details/199496.

32 Omar Ashour, "From Bad Cop to Good Cop: The Challenge of Security Sector Reform in Egypt," *Brookings Doha Center Paper Series* no. 3 (November 2012), http://www.brookings.edu/~/media/Research/Files/Papers/2012/11/19%20security%20sector%20reform%20ashour/Omar%20Ashour%20English.pdf.

33 Egypt 2012 OSAC Crime and Safety Report."

34 Ashour, "Finishing the Job".

35 African Development Bank Group, "Libya Economic Outlook," http://www.afdb.org/en/countries/north-africa/libya/libya-economic-outlook/; Mustafa Fetouri, "What did Libyans gain from the Revolution," *Al-Monitor*, February 24, 2015, http://www.al-monitor.com/pulse/originals/2015/02/libya-after-revolution-social-economy-political-gaddafi.html.

36 U.S. Department of State, "Libya Travel Warning," Jan. 20, 2015, http://travel.state.gov/content/passports/english/alertswarnings/libya-travel-warning.html.

37 Conway Waddington, "The arms proliferation threat of post-Gaddafi Libya," *Consultancy Africa Intelligence Discussion Papers*, December 19, 2011, http://www.consultancyafrica.com/index.php?option=com_content&view=article&id=917:the-arms-proliferation-threat-of-post-gaddafi-libya-&catid=60:conflict-terrorism-discussion-papers&Itemid=265.

38 *BBC News*, "Guide to key Libyan militias and other armed groups," November 23, 2013, http://www.bbc.com/news/world-middle-east-19744533.

39 Fetouri, "What did Libyans gain from the Revolution."

40 Wissam Mata, "Libya: The State of Militias," *Jadaliyya*, Jan. 2, 2014, http://www.jadaliyya.com/pages/index/15847/ليبيا-دولة-الميليشيات.

41 Tom Stevenson, "Tunisian economy awaits its own revolution," *Middle East Eye*, October 25, 2014: http://www.middleeasteye.net/in-depth/features/tunisian-economy-awaits-its-own-revolution-128674744.

DOI: 10.1057/9781137504081.0006

42   Tom Stevenson, "Tunisian economy awaits its own revolution," *Middle East Eye*, Feb. 13, 2015, http://www.middleeasteye.net/in-depth/features/tunisian-economy-awaits-its-own-revolution-128674744.

43   U.S. Department of State, "Tunisia 2015 OSAC Crime and Safety Report," https://www.osac.gov/pages/ContentReportDetails.aspx?cid=17374.

44   Ashour, "Finishing the Job."

45   *The Economist*, "Terror at the Bardo," March 21, 2015, http://www.economist.com/news/middle-east-and-africa/21646786-gunmen-strike-only-democracy-emerge-arab-spring-terror.

46   Human Rights Watch, "World Report 2015 – Syria," http://www.hrw.org/world-report/2015/country-chapters/syria.

47   United Nations High Commissioner for Refugees, "2015 UNHCR country operations profile – Syrian Arab Republic," http://www.unhcr.org/pages/49e486a76.html.

48   Scott Lucas, "Syria Document: UN Report on the Devastation of an 'Economy of Violence," *EA WorldView*, March 16, 2015, http://eaworldview.com/2015/03/syria-document-un-report-on-the-devastation-of-an-economy-of-violence/.

49   An Employee of the *New York Times* in Syria and Damien Cave, "Crime Wave Engulfs Syria as Its Cities Reel From War," *New York Times*, August 9, 2012, http://www.nytimes.com/2012/08/10/world/middleeast/crime-wave-engulfs-syria-as-its-cities-reel-from-war.html?pagewanted=all&_r=0.

50   Scott Lucas, "Syria Document: UN Report on the Devastation of an 'Economy of Violence." : http://eaworldview.com/2015/03/syria-document-un-report-on-the-devastation-of-an-economy-of-violence/

51   Louay Hussein, "The Syrians do not feel the need to the state," *Al-Hayat*, June 24, 2014, http://www.alhayat.com/Opinion/Writers/3167677/ ال-نويروسلا-ىلإ-مهتجاحب-نورعشي.ةلودلا.

52   *The Economist*, "The pushback," March 21, 2015, http://www.economist.com/news/briefing/21646752-sustaining-caliphate-turns-out-be-much-harder-declaring-one-islamic-state-not.

53   Ilina Angelova, " Governance in rebel-held East Ghouta in the Damascus Province, Syria," Center for Governance and Human Rights Working Paper # 10, October 2014, https://www.repository.cam.ac.uk/handle/1810/246194.

54   *European Commission*, "EU leaders agree actions to tackle Mediterranean tragedy," April 24, 2015, http://ec.europa.eu/news/2015/04/20150424_en.htm.

55   Borzou Daragahi, "Libya's border security struggles against people smugglers," *Financial Times*, November 28, 2013, http://www.ft.com/intl/cms/s/0/88a04838-51f2-11e3-8c42-00144feabdc0.html#axzz2uAIdVoDk.

DOI: 10.1057/9781137504081.0006

3

Outward-Directed Security Threats

Abstract: *This chapter addresses the outward-directed threats (e.g., illegal migration, refugees, the use of force, and terrorism). It shows how the "authority vacuum" created by the Arab Spring revolutions has enabled these threats to emerge, while adding the role of those targeted by these threats, that is, the outside world, particularly the immediate neighborhood of the Mediterranean and Southern Europe. In particular, the inability to enable smooth regime transitions from Iraq to Libya to Syria should cause Middle Eastern, European, and US decision-makers to pause and examine alternative approaches. The calls for adapting hard power diplomacy and defense capabilities were answered to a certain extent in the Obama presidential administration and the European Union. However, in recognition of the "original sin," this chapter examines how problems of economic and political development, institution and state building, rule of law and reconciliation, governance and civil society have been dealt with so far.*

Yossef, Amr and Joseph R. Cerami. *The Arab Spring and the Geopolitics of the Middle East: Emerging Security Threats and Revolutionary Change.* Basingstoke: Palgrave Macmillan, 2015. DOI: 10.1057/9781137504081.0007.

DOI: 10.1057/9781137504081.0007

This chapter addresses outward-directed threats in the Middle East, including, the use of force, terrorism, weapons of mass destruction proliferation, as well as human security issues, such as illegal immigration, refugees and violence against noncombatants, especially women and children. The analysis in this threat assessment complements the monograph's earlier argument of how the "authority vacuums" created by the Arab Spring revolutions have enabled these threats to emerge and expand, while adding the role of those targeted by these threats, that is, the regional players, particularly the immediate neighborhood of the Mediterranean and Southern Europe.

A starting assumption for this chapter is that there is a continuing gap between the academic and practitioner ideas, approaches and forecasts. The intellectual anchor then for this chapter is the notion that responding to outward directed threats requires thoughtful analysis and judgment to develop sound strategies.[1] Sound strategies should also look to bridge the gaps that exist among scholars and practitioners. In his literature review essay of the big ideas on post-Cold War international relations by scholars Huntington, Fukuyama and Mearsheimer, professor and former practitioner Richard Betts gets to the essence of the theory-practice divide. While emphasizing the need for ideas for informed policy and decision-making Betts writes that:

> Reminders of the limits of theory ring true to practical people. But if causes and effects are hopelessly random, then there is no hope for informed policy. Terminal uncertainty, however, is not an option for statesmen. They cannot just take shots in the dark, so they cannot do without some assumptions about how the world works. This is why practical people are slaves of defunct economists or contemporary political theorists. Policymakers need intellectual anchors if they are to make informed decisions that are any more likely to move the world in the right direction than the wrong one.[2]

In particular, the failure to enable smooth transitions between regimes, from Iraq to Libya to Egypt to Syria, should cause Middle Eastern, European, US and international scholars and decision-makers to pause and consider alternative approaches. The calls for adapting hard power diplomacy and defense capabilities were answered to a certain extent in the policy statements of the Obama presidential administration as well as European Union officials. However, in recognition of the "original sin" regarding the flaws in the founding and development of the Arab states, as mentioned earlier in this monograph, this chapter will examine problems being faced today in terms of the threats to economic and

DOI: 10.1057/9781137504081.0007

political development, institution and state building, rule of law and reconciliation, governance and civil society.

The father of post-World War II European institution building, Jean Monnet, was inspired by a story about Ibn Saud's secret for success. Ibn Saud is reported to have said: "God appeared to me when I was a young man, and said something which has guided my actions throughout my life. He told me: 'For me, everything is a means – even obstacles.'"[3] It is an open question as to whether the aftermath of the 2011 events will lead to a renaissance in Arab "good government" or continue along a path of autocratic leaders and failing efforts at "state building."

For the West, the United States and the European Union, with their guiding democratic traditions and institutions, there are further questions. For instance, can the Western response to the threats of Middle Eastern political instability and disorder provide the means to improve efforts at state building in influencing, in positive directions, both state capacity and political legitimacy? Or is the nature of the threats is such that there is no viable alternative to the ascendance of autocratic governance, and prevail arguments for stability and security over meaningful reforms that include the rule of law, civil society and legitimate governance? In the introduction to Monnet's *Memoirs*, former US diplomat George Ball points out that: "Optimism to Jean Monnet is the only serviceable hypothesis for a practical man or woman with a passionate desire to get things done" (*Monnet, Memoirs*, p. 14). This analysis then starts with a sense of optimism that must be tempered with a grounded assessments of threats – to help focus the attention of scholars and practitioners on the question of what is to be done in light of the enormous challenges facing the US, EU and of course the Middle Eastern states engaged in creating a sense of order in an increasingly disordered and chaotic region.

3.1   Mediterranean regional threats: since the 2011 Arab Spring: US perspectives

This analysis begins by examining the post Arab Spring events from the perspective of critical threats from both US and European perspectives. The main areas for defining the nature of critical threats include the use of force, expanding terrorist actions, the proliferation of weapons of mass destruction, and human security. The US government's threat perceptions are readily available in open source unclassified documents.

DOI: 10.1057/9781137504081.0007

For instance, US regional perspectives on Middle East and North Africa threats are highlighted publically in official documents published by the Director of National Intelligence and available over the internet.[4] The section on regional threats includes a listing by country, but does not include an overall regional analysis. In terms of the "use of force" in the region it is extraordinary to consider how many wars are ongoing. Conventional, unconventional and now hybrid conflicts, including potential interstate wars and ongoing civil wars, threaten regional as well as global stability.

It is difficult to think of a period of post-World War II history when any region has experienced such extensive warfare, except possibly for Southeast Asia during the US's 25-year war in Vietnam. Currently Iraq, Syria, Libya and Yemen are all engaged in open warfare. A Brookings Institution study points out that Syria is more than "just a civil war" and is now the "central battle in the conflict over a new order in the Middle East."[5] The long-term human costs continue to raise international attention but little action to stop the horrific violence. The ramifications of the civil war, usually characterised as a power struggle between the pro-regime and anti-Assad forces, go well beyond the internal dynamics to include both regional and great power implications.[6]

In Iraq there are currently "lines" of territorial control between Iraqi forces and the Islamic State of Iraq and the Levant (ISIL). Military forces, with army ground forces and militias, supported by air forces, and artillery weapons are competing for territory in conventional ways that would be familiar to all who have studied warfare. ISIL proclaims its intent to expand into the Arabian peninsula and North Africa and challenges both modern Middle Eastern regimes as well as western interests. In Libya rival militias are fighting a civil war that has fractured the political environment and the potential to form a "unity" government.[7] The ethnosectarian conflict in Iraq among the Sunni and Shi'a forces is replicated in Yemen with the Shi'a Huthi battling Al-Qaida (AQAP) as well as Saudi Arabia and its emerging coalition in the Arabian Peninsula.

Supporting the use of force in each of these conflicts are the US and Iran. The Iranian support to Baghdad and Damascus includes arms, advisers, funds and direct combat support.[8] The role of Iran then as a patron state will add capabilities to engage conventional forces as well as the terrorist groups. The extent to which Iran will be willing to provide, or in some case expand, advanced military weaponry, advice and training to the conflicting parties will remain threatening to the region. Examples of the potential for arms transfers would include Iranian sophisticated long range missiles, that US intelligence claims have the range to strike as far away as Southeastern Europe.[9] The growing Iranian expertise in training Arab forces in counterinsurgency, conventional and hybrid warfare, all widens the opportunities to expand regional warfare.

The threat of terrorism continues to spread in a variety of patterns. For instance, the morphing of ISIL into a force that can control large areas inside of and between nation states is a relatively new phenomenon. Add to that the extensive threats of ISIL trained and now battle experienced European and North American individuals provide additional gateways to spread terrorism inside of Western countries. Other complicating patterns are the new inroads into Lebanon, by the Sunni Al Nusrah Front and ISIL in partnership in fighting against the Lebanese Army and the Iranian backed Shi'a Hezbollah. The Syria-Lebanon border area then potentially becomes ungovernable space and an area that can serve as an effective terrorist base.

The Egyptian Sinai is another example of the growing capacity of terrorist groups to find bases in remote areas. Since the Arab Spring and markedly since 2013, the ABM group has become affiliated with IS. The ABM terrorists now claim "responsibility for some of the most sophisticated and deadly attacks against Egyptian security forces in decades."[10] The expansion and deadliness of these terrorist groups is likely to grow without effective and sustained counterterrorist training, doctrine and operations conducted by a strong state with a skilled professional military.

The recent announcement of the US renewing $1.3 billion in annual military aid to the Egyptian government under President el-Sisi is intended to meet the "strategic objectives of both countries in combating terrorism and extremism and maintaining security," particularly in Egypt's restive Sinai Peninsula.[11] This US decision is noteworthy in that reports indicate that the Obama Administration withdrew its earlier certification requirement, that Sissi's government had "made advances in democracy, human rights and rule of law." It is also noteworthy that the aid consists of conventional arms, including orders for 12 F-16 jet aircraft, 20 missiles and 125 M1A1Abrams tank kits. The National Security Council spokeswoman Bernadette Meehan stated specifically that the aid is intended for a "secure and stable Egypt and the defeat of terrorist organizations."[12] However, the press releases from the

DOI: 10.1057/9781137504081.0007

US still stress concerns about "upholding human rights and fundamental freedoms."[13]

Communitarian Amitai Etzioni's ideas regarding the principle of security as a higher priority than democratization provides a logic for understanding the US position with respect to Egypt.[14] Bluntly stated, Etzioni's proposition is that security must be a higher priority than democratic governance. "In short," he summarizes that "moral arguments and empirical evidence support the same proposition: in circumstances under which a full spectrum of rights cannot be advanced simultaneously – a common situation – basic security must lead."[15] From a practitioner's perspective, long-time US career diplomat Ambassador, Frank Wisner validates Etzioni's ideas regarding the need for rethinking the past decade of American policy errors in using abstract goals such as democratization as a framework for defining US national interests in the Middle East. These views could accommodate the Obama Administration's compromise and relative backtracking from its earlier position.

Etzioni is pessimistic about the prevention of what he terms "small-scale terrorism" and encourages differentiating between small-scale and "massive terrorism, which involves WMD" (Etzioni, Security First, p. 216). In his concluding chapter, Etzioni recommends "A Distinct Approach: Deproliferation" with six specific policy recommendations.[16] These recommendations will, as he acknowledges, calls for major efforts by the nuclear nations and regional powers that requires the gradual shift of prevailing norms, economic resources and political capital.

The threat of nuclear weapons of mass destruction continues to dominate headlines, even after the 2015 nuclear agreement between the P5+1 and Iran.[17] Regarding Iran's nuclear programs, former US diplomat, William F. Burns, reminds us that we live in an imperfect world and we have to consider the realities of the world as it is in all of its complexity. In brief, Burns argues that WMD proliferation threats do not have expiration dates and sunset clauses. Like the continued conflicts with the Soviet Union during Cold War arms control negotiations and treaties, Burns reminds us that the Middle East remains in "deep disarray" and there is no reason to expect an "overnight transformation" from Iran's current posture as a "revolutionary, regionally disruptive force."[18] Rather than being transfixed by the recent announcements then, the WMD threats remain of concern. The Pakistani, North Korean and Russian loose nukes threats remain, as do the possibilities for reducing the

DOI: 10.1057/9781137504081.0007

vulnerabilities through reforms in the Nuclear Nonproliferation Treaty.[19] Even under the agreement, the potential for Iran's pursuit of its nuclear program, as well as the safety and security of the nuclear weapons and fissile materials in the stockpiles of the other regional nuclear states, remains a threat to continue to watch closely.

Official US government policy statements have longstanding concerns regarding the nuclear and other regional threats. For instance the US Department of Defense's *Quadrennial Defense Review 2014* points to Iran defying international law and pursuit of capabilities to develop nuclear weapons: "Even as Iran pledges not to pursue nuclear weapons, Iran's other destabilizing activities will continue to pose a threat to the Middle East," especially to US regional allies and partners.[20] Given the past three decades of conflict between the US and Iran, including the more recent imposition of sanctions by the US and the European Union, it will take time and effort to build trust for more cooperation. In the meantime, it will be prudent to consider Iran as a threat in the forms of nuclear proliferation and terrorism as well as its potential to assist in using conventional and unconventional military forces in activities that threaten US and European regional allies and partners, including Saudi Arabia, Jordan and Israel. To continue this analysis, the threats to states should be supplemented with the threats to the people in the conflict zones and the ideas addressed in the concept of human security.

Speaking in Indonesia, in February 2008, Secretary of Defense Robert Gates stressed the need for "new thinking" from traditional national or military security towards a focus on humanitarian elements in both foreign and defense policy:

> What we have seen in Asia in recent years is a very real shift that reflects new thinking in U.S. defense strategy overall. A shift away from the permanent presence of, and direct action by, U.S. forces – and toward the building of the capacity of partners to better defend themselves. A shift away from conventional military deterrence as traditionally understood – think of mechanized divisions poised along the Korean demilitarized zone or the central plains of Germany. A shift toward a mix of the so-called 'hard' and 'soft' elements of national power – where military, diplomatic, economic, cultural, and humanitarian elements are integrated in an effort to ensure long-term security based on our own capabilities but also on the enhanced capabilities of our partners.[21]

Defining the human security dimensions of national security policy and strategy remains unfinished business, of course. The Secretary of Defense

DOI: 10.1057/9781137504081.0007

called for learning lessons from ongoing operations and appreciating the significance of the non-military dimensions of policymaking "beyond security." Gates continues to argue that

> Iraq and Afghanistan remind us that military success alone is insufficient to achieve victory. We must not forget our hard-learned lessons or allow the important soft power capabilities developed because of them to atrophy or even disappear. Beyond security, essential ingredients of long-term success include economic development, institution building, and the rule of law, as well as promoting internal reconciliation, good governance, providing basic services to the people, training and equipping indigenous military and police forces, strategic communications.[22]

Most importantly, the calls for US national security reform and "whole of government" approaches for tackling current and future complex contingencies also demands attention.[23] The US human security agenda includes political, economic and social development as well as the use of armed forces for humanitarian operations.

The pivot in the US focus from the hard power military interventions of the George W. Bush administration, toward the soft or civilian power focus of Barack Obama's administration is captured in another official document, the *2010 Quadrennial Diplomacy and Development Review (QDDR)*. The clear intent of using a policy document to steer US efforts towards human security is this cosponsored, first ever review by the US Department of State and United Stated Agency for International Development. The document's title "Leading Through Civilian Power," is a clear indictor of Secretaries Robert Gates and Hillary Clinton's redirection of US foreign policy towards human security concerns. The next section of this review addresses the threat of failing to meet the human security needs of the populations subjected to "weak governments and failing states."[24]

The analysis points to the security threat that failed states "create safe havens for terrorists, insurgencies, and criminal syndicates."[25] Tensions and disruptions to economies and supply routes can "escalate to mass atrocities and undermine US values including democracy and human rights. Thus the human security focus includes the US "Embracing Conflict Prevention and Response Within Fragile States as a Core Civilian Mission."[26] These tasks include assisting in promoting development, protecting human rights and providing for people as well as supporting the building of government institutions that provide "basic but effective security and justice systems." Good governance and human security then

DOI: 10.1057/9781137504081.0007

go hand-in-hand and are the basis for a US role in both state-building as well as humanitarian operations in response to "disasters, famines, disease outbreaks, and other natural phenomena." Thus the plight of Syria's four million refugees and their impact on the governments and populations of US partners, Jordan, Lebanon, Turkey and Iraq all become part of the puzzle for assessing the threatening nature of not emphasizing human security. The larger issues linking political, economic and social changes brought about by global communications technology as well as markets should also be considered.

Joseph Nye provides a more recent review of the interconnectedness of these new, emerging threats on a regional as well as a global level. Nye writes of the diffusion of power in the 21st century fostering "transnational issues like financial stability, climate change, terrorism, and pandemics."[27] These transnational threats include non-state actors with no regard for national borders that threaten individuals and institutions. The specific non-military threats to individuals are an expansive list including: bankers' electronic funds; hackers threatening cyber security; pandemics; and climate change (Nye, *Is the American Century Over*, p. 96). Recent history in the Middle East, as well as Africa, provides a testament to the validity of Nye's concerns.

Specifically, Nye addresses the Middle East turmoil. He notes the UN Arab Human Development Report that shows "a region that lagged in literacy, science, non-energy trade and information" as "ripe for disruption" (Ibid., p. 106). His pessimistic projection is that the region's information revolution coupled with religious and political disruptions may last for a generation and compares to the regional conflicts in Europe during the Thirty Years' War in the 17th century. In conclusion, Nye points out that the US will not be able to use military forces to occupy and control the nationalistic populations sparked by the dramatic events of the Arab Spring. The threats to human security in issues regarding the internet, climate change, and financial stability require new approaches. In particular, he challenges the US to consider efforts to "shape the international environment and create incentives for others though trade, finance, culture, and institutions. He cites former World Bank president Robert Zoellick's argument that "there are opportunities today to adapt the world to America's benefit that do not involve US military force" (Ibid., p. 124). These opportunities will be strengthened through an agenda of "security first," as Etzioni argues, but most profitably considered as human security as well as state security issues.

DOI: 10.1057/9781137504081.0007

3.2   Mediterranean regional threats: since the 2011 Arab Spring: European perspectives

Like the US government, the European Union official publications provide insights on pre and post-Arab Spring, Middle Eastern threats. Starting with the 2003 European Security Strategy (ESS) document, which was reviewed in 2008, the European Council, which provided the conceptual framework for the Common Security and Defence Policy (CSDP) identifies five key threats, as follows:

1   Terrorism
2   Proliferation of weapons of mass destruction (WMD)
3   Regional conflicts
4   State failure
5   Organized crime.[28]

The EU elaborate organizational structures and accompanying statements reflect deeply the European approach to institution building. Established recently, in 2011, under the Treaty of Lisbon (2009), the European External Action Service (EEAS) is the EU's diplomatic service that combines both foreign and security policy under a High Representative, currently Federica Mogherini of Italy. The EU's founding Treaty principles reflects a liberal internationalist perspective as well as an emphasis on human security:

> Formally launched on 1 January 2011, the Service was created by the Treaty of Lisbon, which itself entered into force in 2009. The principles guiding the EU's activity abroad are defined in the Treaty: The Union's action on the international scene shall be guided by the principles which have inspired its own creation, development and enlargement, and which it seeks to advance in the wider world: democracy, the rule of law, the universality and indivisibility of human rights and fundamental freedoms, respect for human dignity, the principles of equality and solidarity, and respect for the principles of the United Nations Charter and international law.[29]

Founding principles are of course essential for understanding the nature of the EU and its supporting organizational structures, policies and programs. The EU Council's 2008 review "Report on the Implementation of the Initial 2003 European Security Strategy"[30] is also significant as a reflection of the continuity and changes in European threat perceptions. For instance, the 2008 Implementation Report suggests that the EU remains an "anchor of stability" for the continent and forglobal security. Additionally, the report

DOI: 10.1057/9781137504081.0007

suggests the effectiveness of the neighborhood policy[31] and the framework of the southern and eastern partners. The Report highlights the important new dimension provided by the Union of the Mediterranean as helping to respond to emerging and complex threats ("Report on the Implementation of the European Security Strategy," pp. 1, 6). It should be noted that the Union highlights a number of key initiative that address environment, economic, transportation and other issues, but does not emphasize issues related to security threats.[32] In particular, one explicit 2008 policy statement has not stood up well over time: "Threat or use of military force cannot be allowed to solve territorial issues – anywhere" ("Report on the Implementation of the European Security Strategy," p. 2). That said, the report makes no reference to concerns about conventional or civil wars in Europe's Mediterranean neighborhood.

The 2008 Report points to the proliferation of weapons of mass destruction as the number one security threat (Ibid., p. 3). The threats from Iran and North Korea are highlighted. Iran is portrayed as a danger to regional stability as well as to the "whole non-proliferation system" (Ibid., p. 1). The pressing concerns for Nonproliferation Treaty reform, as well as for establishing the updated rules needed in expectation of an increasing demand for civilian nuclear power deserve more attention. Specific concerns are those of a technical nature, including the "nuclear fuel cycle, countering financing of proliferation; measures on bio-safety and bio-security; containing proliferation of delivery systems, notably ballistic missiles;" as well as calling for a multilateral treaty "banning the production of fissile material for nuclear weapons" (Ibid., p. 3).

In 2008, terrorism and organized crime were listed as the number two threat facing the European Union. Then the policy prescription included more organizational responses, including the appointment of EU counterterrorism coordinators, constructing crisis coordination and civil protection mechanisms (Ibid., p. 4). The EU also highlights initiatives for great multilateralism, especially with the United Nations. The UN's "Alliance of Civilizations" is promoted and continues the work started in 2005 by Secretary General Kofi Anan and sponsored by the governments of Spain and Turkey.

The United Nations Alliance of Civilizations is "A High-Level Group of experts was formed by Mr. Annan to explore the roots of polarization between societies and cultures today, and to recommend a practical program of action to address this issue."[33] The current director, or High Representative, has addressed the linkages among development and

DOI: 10.1057/9781137504081.0007

global security: "He re-iterated on several occasions that peace, security, human rights and development are mutually re-enforcing elements; without peace there will be no chance for development. He firmly believes that building tolerance, respecting diversity and promoting co-existence is a moral obligation if we want to advance the causes of peace, human rights and development."[34]

The recent 2015 global forums provide opportunities to discuss initiatives to reduce tensions, but the implementation and effectiveness of the UNAOC and other multilateral agencies is clearly a work in progress. The High Representative in March 2015 strikes the right chords in terms of aspirations for promoting a "global, collective security architecture with a clear role for regional arrangements."[35] Given the events of the Arab Spring as well as the ongoing Middle Eastern conflicts, the summary from the 2008 Implementation Report rings true in 2015 – in that "Progress has been slow and incomplete" ("Report on the Implementation of the European Security Strategy," p. 4).

Gaps between the other aspirations between 2008 and 2015 remain interesting for comparison purposes in term of contrasting goals with policy implementation. For instance, in 2008, with the formation of the Union for the Mediterranean, there was more emphasis on diplomacy and development than on military operations, civil wars and terrorism. The Implementation Report suggests the effectiveness of European diplomacy in the Israel-Palestine conflict due to the potential of the Quartet, including the EU, UN, US and Russian Federation.[36] Additional initiatives include the relationship linking development to state fragility; maritime safety; energy; water; and migration etc. ("Report on the Implementation of the European Security Strategy," p. 10).

Jumping from 2008 to 2015, the Council on Foreign Relations (CFR) has a positive review titled the "European Agenda on Security," published on January 11, 2015. Here again the CFR positively summarizes the European Union's "actions, measures and initiatives" to fight terrorism in particular. The elevation of the terrorist threat and the European Commission's counterterrorism efforts are addressed as ready for adoption in 2015 to provide a "focus for security priorities during 2015–2020."[37] Again the EU's legal-structural preferences are related in a CFR overview that stresses the EU's organizational and process priorities including: an "Internal Security Strategy;" the "Schengen Information System" or "Civil Protection Mechanism;" the "Radicalization Awareness Network;" and the "US Terrorist Finance Tracking Program." The CFR overview includes links to the EU security strategies of 2003 and 2010. What the CFR overview and the EU fact sheet of the European Agenda on

DOI: 10.1057/9781137504081.0007

Security do not clearly reflect is an assessment of successes and failures of the strategies in terms of the events that led to the Arab Spring or the impact of the Union for the Mediterranean and other neighborhood policies in the pre and post Arab Spring periods. In essence, there is a question of the need for a comprehensive performance review that assesses whether the previous attempts, policies, strategies, processes and organizations effectively identify threats and respond with effective security policies.

Two European centers have reviewed the EU's performance and provide very critical assessments. The Centre for European Policy Studies, in cooperation with the Friedrich Ebert Stiftung, in February 2015, asserts that emergencies, hybrid threats, defense spending cuts, and evolving global trends "have all eroded the EU's role as a security action in a multipolar world."[38] They suggest that reforms are urgently needed in strategy, institutional capabilities, and resources, noting that the Common Security and Defence Policy (CSDP) requires serious reform. They conclude that in view of the "grave threats" to European security and defense, a more efficient and effective framework requires taking "bold and concrete steps" (Ibid., p. 17).

A similar review by the Bertelsmann Stiftung is equally critical of the European Union's neighborhood strategy. The title of their study "The EU Neighbourhood in Shambles" certainly telegraphs their main finding.[39] In a sharply pointed critique, they contend that the "arc of instability" from the EU's eastern borders to the Mediterranean basin "has undermined its flagship European Neighbourhood Policy (ENP)." They conclude that the ENP "has manifestly failed and needs to be radically rethought." Their call is for "transformational change" with a "wider range of actors, including civil society, promote entrepreneurship and help reform countries' police and military forces." Given what has transpired in the EU in policy, strategy, and institution building prior to the shocking events of the Arab Spring then, to paraphrase Lenin: "What is to be done?"

The next chapter will offer suggestions for improving the Mediterranean regional security of the US and Europe as well as the Middle East and North Africa states that will require a collaborative effort – to improve their effectiveness for aligning and integrating the diplomacy, defense and development necessary in diplomatic negotiations, conventional wars, counterterrorism, stability and reconstruction efforts, foreign aid programs, humanitarian relief operations and ultimately to promote human security.

DOI: 10.1057/9781137504081.0007

Integrating the instruments of power for state and regional security in the case of the recent revolutions in MENA will not be an easy goal. That, however, does not address the ends of a new policy based on critical theory and human security. For insights on the overarching policy objectives we can return to President Obama's own words in his Cairo speech in 2009. He called for a "new beginning" that emphasizes "common principles of justice and progress; tolerance and the dignity of all human beings."[40] The speech goes on to address many of the issues identified in critical theory in the early sections of this paper. Whether the US can substantially implement the 3D's of diplomacy, defense and development, and assist in building regional and state security given the current geopolitics of the Middle East, in new and creative ways to address the issues of the Arab Spring, remains to be seen. The ability of the US and other actors to respond to the threats created by or related to the revolutions of the Arab Spring remains a work in progress that must link theory and practice, and convert ideas into action. As Henry Kissinger concludes in his book *Diplomacy,* as the Spanish proverb points out: "Traveler... there are no roads. Roads are made by walking."[41]

Notes

1   For a fuller discussion of "threat" as an external determinant (along with considerations of geography and technology) for designing strategy, see Aaron L. Friedberg, *In the Shadow of the Garrison State: America's Anti-Statism and Its Cold War Grand Strategy* (Princeton: Princeton University Press, 2000), p. 64.

2   Richard K. Betts, "Conflict or Cooperation?" in *The Clash at 20: What did Samuel P. Huntington's "Clash of Civilizations?" get right and wrong, and how does it look two decades later?* (Foreign Affairs, New York: Council on Foreign Relations, 2013), p. 79.

3   This story is cited widely. See for instance Pascal Menoret, *The Saudi Enigma: A History* (New York: Palgrave Macmillan, 2005), p. 117. See also Jean Monnet, *Memoirs* (New York: Doubleday & Company, Inc., 1978), p. 799.

4   James R. Clapper, Director of National Intelligence, "Statement for the Record: Worldwide Threat Assessment of the US intelligence Community, Senate Armed Services Committee," February 26, 2015. This document's beginning section categorizes global threats in terms of: cyber, counterintelligence, terrorism, weapons of mass destruction and proliferation, space and counterspace, transnational organized crime, economics and natural resources, and human security.

DOI: 10.1057/9781137504081.0007

5   "Big Bets, Black Swans: A Presidential Briefing Book; Policy
     Recommendations for President Obama in 2014," (Washington, DC: Foreign
     Policy at Brookings, January 2014), p. 21.

6   For a thoughtful critique of the potential for the use of force in Syria see
     Clark A. Murdock, "What Has Syria Taught Us About the Right Time to
     Use Force?" in Craig Cohen, Kathleen Hicks, and Josiane Gabel, ed., *2014
     Global Forecast: U.S. Security Policy at a Crossroads*, CSIS, Center for Strategic &
     International Studies (Lanham: Rowman & Littlefield Publishers, Inc., 2013).

7   Clapper, "Statement for the Record," p. 15.

8   *Ibid.*, p. 14.

9   *Ibid.*

10   Clapper, "Statement for the Record," p. 16.

11   The Associated Press, "US Military Aid Released to Egypt Boosts Leader's
     Legitimacy," *The New York Times*, April 1, 2015 [http://www.nytimes.com/
     aponline/2015/04/01/world/middleeast/ap-ml-egypt-us.html?_r=0].

12   Reuters, "White House lifts hold on military aid to Egypt," March 31, 2015
     [www.jpost.com/Middle-East/White-House-lifts-hold-on-military-aid-to-
     Egypt-395760].

13   Peter Paker, "Obama Removes Weapons Freeze against Egypt," *New York
     Times*, March 31, 2015.

14   Amitai Etzioni, *Security First: For a Muscular, Moral Foreign Policy* (New
     Haven: Yale University Press, 2007). See Ambassador Frank Wisner,
     "US Policy and the Middle East Crisis," UC Berkeley Events, Institute of
     International Studies, March 6, 2015, [http://youtu.be/EqpatojCpeQ].

15   Etzioni, *Security First*, p. 8.

16   A summary of Etzioni's "Deproliferation" concept includes (p. 238):

     a.   Upgrading security at nuclear arms and fissile materials storage facilities
          temporarily until these materials can be blended down or dismantled.
     b.   Expropriating fissile materials to safe havens and blend them down in
          safe havens.
     c.   Replacing all HEU [highly enriched uranium] with LEU [low enriched
          uranium], which in effect cannot be used in making bombs.
     d.   Preventing transnational trade and transportation of nuclear bombs and
          materials.
     e.   Preventing the construction of new facilities that use HEU.
     f.   Offer rogue states non aggression treaties and arrangements for giving
          up their nuclear arms programs.

     Note that Etzioni cites similar proposals from Graham Allison and others
     who study nonproliferation. See Graham Allison's *Nuclear Terrorism: The
     Ultimate Preventable Catastrophe, (*New York: Henry Holt and Company,
     2005). For the authors views on the successes and failures in past US and
     UN counterproliferation efforts, with case studies on Russia and the Former

DOI: 10.1057/9781137504081.0007

Soviet States, North Korea and Iraq, see Joseph R. Cerami, *Leadership and Policy Innovation: Countering the Proliferation of Weapons of Mass Destruction* (New York: Routledge, 2013).

17   The P5+1 refers to the five permanent members of the UN Security Council; the US, China, France Russia and the United Kingdom; plus Germany. Arms Control Association, Fact Sheets and Briefs, "History of Official Proposals on the Iranian Nuclear Issue," January 2014 [http://www.armscontrol.org/factsheets/Iran_Nuclear_Proposals].

18   J. Burns, "The Fruits of Diplomacy With Iran," *The New York Times,* April 2, 2015 [http://www.nytimes.com/2015/04/03/opinion/a-good-deal-with-iran.html?smid=fb-share&_r=2].

19   Burns for example briefly discusses: the "absence of a clear divide between civilian and military programs;" "the gray zone in the treaty between the right to use nuclear energy and the prohibition against manufacturing nuclear weapons;" and the task of "building a sturdy firewall between military and peaceful [nuclear] activities." He places this task in the context of the potential for nuclear energy to reduce greenhouse gas emissions.

20   Chuck Hagel, *2014 Quadrennial Defense Review (QDR),* (Washington: Secretary of Defense, March 4, 2014), p. 5.

21   U.S. Department of Defense, Office of the Assistant Secretary of Defense (Public Affairs), Speech by Secretary of Defense Robert M. Gates, To Indonesian Council on World Affairs, Jakarta, Indonesia, Monday, February 25, 2008 [http://www.america.gov/st/texttrans-english/2008/February/20080225130031eaifaso.2525141.html].

22   Robert M. Gates, 2008, *National Defense Strategy*, p. 17. [http://www.defenselink.mil/news/2008%20National%20Defense%20Strategy.pdf].

23   See efforts for linking State-Defense-USAID efforts through the Consortium for Complex Operations (CCO) [http://ccoportal.org/]. The Center for Complex Operations (CCO) was initially formed in the summer of 2008 in the Office of the Secretary of Defense (Policy) and moved in early 2009 to the National Defense University. The CCO publishes the security studies journal *PRISM.*

24   Hillary Rodham Clinton, *Leading Through Civilian Power: the First Quadrennial Diplomacy and Development Review, Executive Summary* (Washington, DC: US Department of State, 2010), p. 12.

25   *Ibid.*, p. 12.

26   *Ibid.*, p. 13.

27   Joseph S. Nye Jr., *Is the American Century Over?* (Malden, MA: Polity Press), p. 95.

28   See the European Union External Action fact sheet on the European Security Strategy at http://www.eeas.europa.eu/csdp/about-csdp/european-security-strategy/.

DOI: 10.1057/9781137504081.0007

29 See About the European External Action Service (EEAS) at http://www.eeas. europa.eu/background/about/index_en.htm.

30 "Report on the Implementation of the European Security Strategy – Providing g Security in a Changing World," http://www.consilium.europa.eu/ ueDocs/cms_Data/docs/pressdata/EN/reports/104630.pdf.

31 For EU information on the European Neighbourhood Policy see http:// www.eeas.europa.eu/enp/index_en.htm. The Union for the Mediterranean (UfM) formerly known as the Barcelona process includes "15 Southern Mediterranean, African and Middle Eastern countries are members of the UfM: Albania, Algeria, Bosnia and Herzegovina, Egypt, Israel, Jordan, Lebanon, Mauritania, Monaco, Montenegro, Morocco, Palestine, Syria (suspended), Tunisia and Turkey." See the Euro-Mediterranean Partnership (EUROMED) at http://eeas.europa.eu/euromed/index_en.htm.

32 See the Euro-Mediterranean Partnership (EUROMED) at http://eeas.europa. eu/euromed/index_en.htm. Key initiatives include:
   ▸ the de-pollution of the Mediterranean Sea, including coastal and protected marine areas;
   ▸ the establishment of maritime and land highways that connect ports and improve rail connections so as to facilitate movement of people and goods;
   ▸ a joint civil protection programme on prevention, preparation and response to natural and man-made disasters;
   ▸ Mediterranean solar energy plan that explores opportunities for developing alternative energy sources in the region;
   ▸ a Euro-Mediterranean University, inaugurated in Slovenia in June 2008;
   ▸ the Mediterranean Business Development Initiative, which supports small businesses operating in the region by first assessing their needs and then providing technical assistance and access to finance.

33 See the UNAOC: United Nations Alliance of Civilizations at http://www. unaoc.org/who-we-are/.

34 *Ibid.*

35 See Remarks by H.E. Nassir Abdulaziz Al-Nasser, The UN High Representative for the Alliance of Civilizations, "At Mediation in the Mediterranean Seminar", Casa Arabe, Madrid March 17, 2015 at http://www. unaoc.org/2015/03/remarks-by-h-e-nassir-abdulaziz-al-nasser-the-un-high-representative-for-the-alliance-of-civilizations-at-the-mediation-in-the-mediterranean-seminar/.

36 See "The EU and the Middle East Peace Process": http://www.eeas.europa.eu/ mepp/index_en.htmm.

37 "European Agenda on Security: fighting terrorism at EU level, an overview of Commission's actions, measures and initiatives," New York: Council on Foreign Relations," January 11, 2015 at http://www.cfr.org/regional-security/ european-agenda-security/p35993.

DOI: 10.1057/9781137504081.0007

38   "More Union in European Defense: Report of a CEPS Task Force," (Brussels; Centre for European Policy Studies, February 2015).

39   "The EU neighbourhood in shambles: Some recommendations for a new European neighbourhood strategy" (Gutersloh, Germany: Bertelsmann Stiftung, 2015), p. 3.

40   "Text: Obama's Speech in Cairo," *The New York Times*, June 4, 2009 at http://www.nytimes.com/2009/06/04/us/politics/04obama.text. html?pagewanted=all&_r=0.

41   Henry Kissinger, *Diplomacy* (New York: Simon & Schuster, 1994), p. 836.

DOI: 10.1057/9781137504081.0007

4

Redemption? The Geopolitics of MENA and Mediterranean Security

Abstract: *This chapter explains how the future success of the Arab Spring in reaching a modern, democratic states, as well as security of the US, European and other Middle East and North African states will require collaborative efforts to improve their effectiveness for aligning and integrating the necessary diplomacy, defense and development capabilities. Integrating the instruments of power in the case of the recent revolutions in MENA will not be an easy goal. That, however, does not address the ends of a new policy based on critical theory and human security. For insights on the objective we can return to President Obama's own words in his speech in Cairo in 2009. Whether the US can substantially implement the 3D's of diplomacy, defense and development, given the current geopolitics of the Middle East, in new and creative ways to address the issues of the Arab Spring remains the test of US leadership.*

Yossef, Amr and Joseph R. Cerami. *The Arab Spring and the Geopolitics of the Middle East: Emerging Security Threats and Revolutionary Change.* Basingstoke: Palgrave Macmillan, 2015. DOI: 10.1057/9781137504081.0008.

This chapter reflects on the question of "what is to be done" or how the promise of the Arab Spring in the early attempts of reaching goals, such as, enabling the development of modern, democratic states, as well as improving the security of the US, European and other MENA states will require a collaborative effort. No one nation can provide regional security, but it remains possible to improve regional as well as national effectiveness for aligning and integrating the diplomacy, defense and development necessary for national as well as human security in implementing policies, strategies and programs to enhance security, stability and reconstruction at the national and regional levels. No doubt there will be continuing MENA internal and external threats and opportunities that will require extensive diplomatic negotiations, conventional wars, counterterrorism, stability and reconstruction efforts, foreign aid programs and humanitarian relief operations. The notion of redemption is, therefore, dealt with in this chapter in two sections, the first deals with state-building, that is to be done by the Arab Spring countries themselves and the second section is about restoring United States' leadership role in international affairs as well as regional geopolitics. A priority then would be to consider fixing first American national security institutions and policymaking as a precursor for reforming the US's geopolitical approach to MENA regional and national reform efforts.

Redemption from the "original sin," that is the Arab state weakness or failure, requires first recognition of the problem. It is tempting to continue thinking of the Arab Middle East various problems merely as caused by immature cultures, societal divisions and lack of democracy. The result of such analysis would be a continuation of the same policies that led to these very same problems of state weakness or failure. First, this analysis not only has a weaker ground in reality as we have shown in Chapter 1, but also, and more importantly, is solution-crippling. To assume that the leaderships of these countries and the international community could transform, somehow and in a relatively short time, these societies to drastically change their (supposedly anti-reform) cultures, societal divisions and political systems, could mean that neither objective change nor reform could be achieved. Before moving forward, let us review shortly what the literature proposes as policy recommendations to the US and EU on the Arab Spring.

The EU Arab Spring policy has been characterized by a holistic perception of the MENA region based on an analytic study of the

DOI: 10.1057/9781137504081.0008

shortcomings exposed by the Arab pro-democracy revolutions in 2011 in the EU approach to the southern Mediterranean region, mainly the European Neighborhood Policy (ENP). The relevant literature, for instance, refers to "regional socio-economic conditions" and stresses the necessity for the EU to deal with MENA as a whole, proposing "regional strategy."[1]

By no means is the regional approach wrong, given the several "commons" between the Arab Spring countries. At the same time, however, this should not lead to an underestimation of the different internal conditions in each of the Arab countries that have had a significant impact on how the uprising developed and would certainly influence the future political processes. Each country in the region has its own specific characteristics and individual grievances, differing significantly from each other: history and culture, demographic composition, role of the military, resources, and geostrategic situation.

Second, the literature appears to take for granted the transformation of the southern Mediterranean into an East Europe-like region as the aim of the proposed EU strategy. Analogies have been made between the East European revolutions that overthrew the communist regimes and the Arab uprisings.[2] Equally, suggestions were offered, accordingly, to the EU to deal with the current uprisings with the same resolve that was brought to Eastern Europe at the end of the Cold War, identifying "common goals" for the countries facing the difficult post-dictatorship challenges.[3]

This perception, while acknowledging the difference in the EU aims in the two cases – full integration into the EU in the case of East Europe and good neighborhood in the case of MENA – overlooks the apparent dissimilarities between the two regions. These dissimilarities range from the depth of socioeconomic development, liberal tradition in societies, level of education, and most importantly, the relative state strength or weakness in these two regions.

Third, scholars advance almost the same pre-revolutions proposition that is European economic/financial aid to the countries south of the Mediterranean, though in different ways. Seen as the appropriate method to preventing a reactionary backlash that could end up into new dictatorship or extremist regimes instead of democratization, economic/financial aid was proposed either in the form of trade agreements,[4] adoption by Arab states of European-like legislation to facilitate widening trade,[5] or major concessions on market access, financial aid and

DOI: 10.1057/9781137504081.0008

migration policy.[6] This approach, however, is in stark contradiction with these scholars' acknowledgment of the fact that the EU economic crisis imposes significant restraints over its ability to sustain the traditional tool of influence – economic aid. Take for example Uri Dadush's and Michele Dunne's proposal to establish trade agreements between the EU and the Arab countries and Balfour's suggestion to revive the Deep and Comprehensive Free Trade Area (DCFTA) now on offer to all the countries in the EU's neighborhood.[7] Ostensibly, free trade agreements might help remedy the absence of a vibrant private sector in MENA, but they might as well add significantly to the European public debt that is already high in several of the EU member states.

In short, the state of the literature is characterized by three shortcomings that could undermine its attempt to provide practical recommendations to the EU to deal with the Arab revolutions: an inflated focus on the regional approach; a misguided analogy to the East European revolutions; and proposing economic/financial aid that the EU would not be able to provide in a sustainable way.

In recognition of the traditional division of labor between the EU and the United States – that is the former provides economic support while the latter provides political and security support – extant literature has been consistently pushing democracy promotion. However, the experiences of the United States in "engineering" change in post-occupation Afghanistan and Iraq are noteworthy that the hoped-for reform requires both a different analysis that takes into account the root causes of the problem, and a different type of leadership in the United States, as we shall explain in greater detail in the second section of this chapter.

Unfortunately, the sad experience of "premature democratization" as in the cases of Afghanistan and Iraq did not bear a significant impact on the US policy vis-a-vis the Arab Spring, which, caught America in the middle of its "withdrawal" from the region in favor of the Far East. Moreover, the Arab Spring took place under an administration that, as the case of Egypt suggest, has been "wavering" between idealist and pragmatist approaches, but that appears to adopt a democratization-at-all-costs model, like the adoption of the so-called " 'engagement-leads-to-moderation" ' theory according to which, the engagement of Islamists in the political process would transform them from radical groups into moderate forces "since their attempt to get the votes of a large sectors of society would necessarily mean the Islamists' adoption of compromises and ideas that are consistent with what the majority believes in."[8]

DOI: 10.1057/9781137504081.0008

4.1 State-building

It is now almost a fashion to stress institution-building and project management as a way to solve the structural problems that existed for decades in the Third World countries, including the four Arab Spring cases, especially with regards to foreign economic aid since the issue has not always been not the insufficiency of funds but the insufficiency of management and technical expertise, and ill-conceived projects.[9] According to this recipe, the aid of the international community should rather focus on the institution-building and project management, by training and offering consultancy.

A recent important work in this direction is *Why Nations Fail*.[10] Notwithstanding its stress on the institutional factor, it still gave priority to "political inclusiveness," which keeps this important contribution within the limits of the "premature democracy" promotion. Another important work that made a straight argument against "premature democratization" and for institution-building in weak/failed states is *Fixing Fragile States*. Notwithstanding it promising focus, it still repeatedly stresses the social cohesion factor and proposes the solution in "designing institutions around identity groups."[11] At the same time, in retrospect though, the author's recommendation for institution adopted building in Assad's Syria – in which the Assad family voluntarily leaves power to an elected council – would now be over-idealistic.

Notwithstanding the human tragedies involved in almost all the Arab Spring revolutions, the enormous changes that the revolutions brought could also serve as a starting point. Indeed, Joel Migdal had once identified massive societal dislocation, in the form of war, mass migration or revolution, as a necessary condition for creating a strong state; in his view, societies must be weakened before a new distribution of social control is possible.[12] Migdal also identified sufficient conditions for creating a strong state, including world historical timing "in which exogenous political forces favor concentrated social control," military threat, the basis for independent bureaucracy and skillful leadership.[13] Thanks to the well-known strategic repercussions of the Arab Spring, internally and externally, it would not be an exaggeration to consider that a world historical timing and military threats are all fulfilling conditions in today's Arab world, either those countries that have witnessed a revolution and those who have not.

However, for Arab Spring countries, skillful leadership will be key to reform. A prime example of skillful leaders who helped create strong states, which were neither entirely democratic nor socially coherent, is Singapore's Lee Kuan Yew who appears to be a typical model of Migdal's description:

> [S]kilful top leadership must be present to take advantage of the conditions to build a strong state. Rulers must be competent at a number of levels. They must carefully select bureaucrats who can and will proffer strategies of survival to the population based on the principles of leaders. Also, they must have a keen eye toward the changing risk calculus. Leaders must know when to move and against whom; changing conditions demand pragmatism in their approach.[14]

Under Yew's leadership, Singapore achieved a well-sustained "miracle" of economic development and stability, under neither Western-style democracy (in which Kuan Lee saw many flaws) nor social cohesion (until the mid-twentieth century Singapore did not exist as a country, manifesting a polyglot collection of migrants). Instead, the Singaporean model was build upon "meritocracy," or bureaucracy by the most able, efficient and untarnished, that could enforce the law, provide services, and advance development.[15] This example of Singapore, as well as South Africa, share several characteristics with the Arab world, that is, colonization, new state structure, ethnic diversities, though nevertheless divert from the Arab world in the success of their states. These examples should shift the explanatory attention of the absence/presence of a "nation-state" to the absence/presence of "state-nations," were the "nation", in terms of self-conscious identity and cultural integration, was the product of the state and not vice versa in most the post-colonial Third World countries (Kaplan, *Fixing Fragile States*, pp. 28–32).

Needless to say, such skillful leaders cannot be imposed from above. It is the role of societies in Egypt, Tunisia, Libya and Syria, to develop this kind of leader, or otherwise there will be little, if any chance, of success in their absence. We elaborate on the qualities of such a skillful leadership in the next section.

Finally, there is the need for an independent bureaucracy that is "skillful enough to execute the grand designs of state leaders." Based on our analysis of the root causes of the crises in the four Arab Spring countries in Chapter 1, we believe that a considerably pressing mission that the societies of these countries most need is state-building, in the form of a capable bureaucracy that not only monopolizes over the legitimate use of force within the country's territories but also enforces law, delivers services and administers the country in a way that is efficient, just and

DOI: 10.1057/9781137504081.0008

beneficial to its citizens. While it is absolutely important to maintain local ownership of any reform proposal, former, traditional attempts to "reform" the old bureaucracies in weak/failed states have failed thanks to the obstacles faced by the reform-seekers, local and international alike. These obstacles are very close to the obstacles to reforming the security sector in the Arab world, as described in 2013 by Omar Ashour, especially the following: the extreme political polarization that leads to politicization of reform and political violence, internal resistance to reform by the anti-reform elements; and limited government capacity and limited knowledge and experience among those who are supposed to implement reform.[16]

That "reforming" institutions the old way has not worked is not a recommendation for destroying these institutions completely and build from scratch as the United States has done, for example, with the Iraqi army, and even more recently with the Qaddafi's regime, only to regret the consequences shortly later, as manifested in the unprecedented threats of terrorism and illegal migration in Libya following the NATO campaign.[17] Egypt's President Sisi is probably attempting to strike this balance, focusing on state institutions as a priority. In his words:

> It is imperative to preserve state institutions even if they had some negative aspects that will be gradually fixed ... This direction is better compared to the idea of destroying state institutions and re-building them anew, especially that regional circumstances around us [Egypt] provide clear evidence on the important of preserving state institutions.[18]

Fixing state institutions should start with recognition that it was these institutions failure that led to the current situation and they cannot perform better by pouring into them more resources in terms of personnel, budgets or training. The fact that ever since the 1980s, dubbed the "decade of administrative reform," and afterwards, significant efforts and resources have been spent in the Arab world into this particular area, that is building administrative capacity, including reorganization, job description, training, leadership and skills development, performance evaluation, procedural simplification, information system, updating laws, improving coordination, decentralization, definition of objectives, and so on. These efforts have not obviously been successful, because, as Jamil Jerisat explains:

> None of the reform programs reviewed constitutes a mature, coherent strategy carrying the necessary operation thrust. Each is merely a collection of proposed

DOI: 10.1057/9781137504081.0008

medical actions that at best are stopgap measures incapable of addressing the continually worsening problems. In fact, it is justifiable to consider proposed reform remedies as a Band-Air approach to a heavily bleeding patient.[19]

His excellent analysis notwithstanding, Jerisat, like other scholars, eventually sticks to the conventional wisdom's solution of democratizing political change.[20] Instead, the entire setting of these institutions could be changed even without the ideal democratic promotion, which, as the case of Morsi's presidency in Egypt could tell, would not be of much value as the concept of democracy is merely limited to holding free elections. For this particular purpose, the first step in this direction, unfortunately, would have to be neither democratic nor consistent with the existing labor laws. This step that the leader should take is to hire a competent committee, composed both of independent as well insider effective experts, in each large administrative unit. The task of such a committee is to put an overall re-plan of this administrative unit in all its aspects, ranging from assigning a mission to the unit, to job descriptions, to hire-and-fire policies, all within new solid civil-service laws and regulations to guarantee the effectiveness of this unit in fulfilling the role of the "state" in its area of competence, making the state services available and efficient. Simplistic as it may appear, this approach could be the way to guarantee that citizens of the state, paraphrasing the Syrian opposition leader Louay Hussein, "feel" once again their need and loyalty to their state, regardless of how socially cohesive it may be. Political courage is particularly stressed since these measures would almost certainly meet significant opposition from those beneficiary of the status quo. But this is exactly where the good leaders are supposed to fit.

4.2   Restoring America's leadership

4.2.1   Fix America first?

Integrating the instruments of power remains, in the case of the recent revolutions in Middle East and North Africa, an elusive goal. That, however, does not address the ends of a new policy based on critical theory and human security. For insights on the objective we can return to President Obama's own words in his speech in Cairo in 2009. He called for a "new beginning" that emphasizes "common principles of justice and progress; tolerance and the dignity of all human beings." The speech goes on to address many of the issues identified in critical theory in the

DOI: 10.1057/9781137504081.0008

early sections of this paper. Whether the US can substantially implement the 3D's of diplomacy, defense and development, given the current geopolitics of the Middle East, in new and creative ways to address the issues of the Arab Spring remains to be seen. The ability of the US and other actors to respond to the threats created by the revolutions of the Arab Spring remains a work in progress. This section then examines improving the United States ability to assist in improving national and regional security for better aligning and integrating the US's ability to serve as a positive force for improving the geopolitics of the Middle East and North Africa in terms of regional, national and human security in the policy areas of defense, diplomacy and development.

4.2.2   Tales from two cases: effectiveness and ineffectiveness in geopolitics

One need not to look far into history to find examples of the US practicing the kind of leadership that led to successful policymaking and implementation. For instance, the United States and Russia cooperated, in very recent history, in the removal and destruction of weapons of mass destruction. Under what are known as Nunn-Lugar programs, the US has worked closely with Russia, and other countries, in removing weapons of mass destruction with remarkable efficiency and effectiveness. The case of the Syrian chemical weapons removal was certainly informed by this experience that can serve as a guidepost for renewing efforts among the great powers and potentially through the United Nations Security Council for countering WMD and other threats in the MENA region. Let us review the highlights of what is arguably the most successful regional security program of the post-Cold War era.[21]

The efforts by Senators Sam Nunn (Democrat of Georgia) and Richard Lugar (Republican of Indiana) in US-Russian Cooperative Threat Reduction Programs were key to the effectiveness of the Counterproliferation Policy Initiative that was launched during the first Clinton Administration. Government policymakers, national security experts, scientists and engineers were among the first to seize the opportunity for forming new relationships among the United States, Russia, and the former Soviet republics (FSR) following the fall of the Berlin Wall in 1989. Initially, President George H.W. Bush's notion of a new world order[22] was significant for the executive branch and especially the State and Defense Departments' promotion of new initiatives. In the following Clinton administration, in reflecting on his experiences as Secretary of Defense,

DOI: 10.1057/9781137504081.0008

William Perry notes the significance of the post-Cold War period for establishing an "effective U.S. partnership with Russia in the security sphere." In their history of these early counter-proliferation programs, defense department officials, Ashton Carter (the current Secretary of Defense) and William Perry (Clinton's first Secretary of Defense, now with the Hoover Institution at Stanford University) point to the early post-Cold War discussions urging Russia's policy elite to become "integrationists" to achieve a new, "self-respecting place in the world order."

In their book, *Preventive Defense,* Carter and Perry discuss early administration approaches and their experiences as Defense Department officials in the first Clinton administration.[23] The George Bush (41) and then Clinton administrations, in supporting Senators Nunn and Lugar's initiative, responded quickly to the new threat of nuclear armed former Soviet republics. Under the authorizing Nunn-Lugar legislation, Defense Department policymakers addressed "loose nukes" issues with programs to eliminate nuclear weapons and fissile material in the Ukraine, and then in Kazakhstan, and Belarus. Special projects, such as Project Sapphire removed weapons grade plutonium and enriched uranium from Kazakhstan and included internal US collaboration among the Departments of Defense, Energy, State, and the CIA.

Other factors in the Nunn-Lugar bargaining do stand out. Traditional Cold War concerns about security and secrecy had to be overcome. Information about compliance arrangements was crucial for building trust and confidence for continuing the program. The complexity and high degree of transparency necessary insured that each side had to step up to new challenges for continuing to shape a new post-Cold War relationship.

There is a real case to be made to emphasize in the Syrian WMD disarmament project for promoting legal norms, legitimate claims and preferences for positive interactions and change. Early Nunn-Lugar barriers included overcoming fifty years of Cold War mistrust with the Russians. Carter and Perry's account includes the significance of President Clinton and Vice President Gore's interventions to develop trust with the new governments of Russia, Ukraine, Kazakhstan and Belarus. The Nunn-Lugar programs successes were tied to the larger issues regarding building a community of shared norms, values and identities in terms of international institutions, arms control and multilateral organizations.

Carter and Perry do note some of the costs and consequences of Nunn-Lugar Cooperative Threat Reductions Programs in terms of budgetary issues and performance results. For instance, they highlight $2.4 billion in

DOI: 10.1057/9781137504081.0008

funding as of mid-1998. They go on to point to the success of 40 engineering projects in Russia to build safeguards for existing stockpiles, dismantle weapons and missiles and convert defense industry to civilian purposes. Carter and Perry also write of the success of destroying 4800 nuclear weapons, removing nuclear weapons from all non-Russian former Soviet republics and eliminating proliferation threats in Belarus, Kazakhstan and the Ukraine. Perry and Carter stress that they "never expected this astounding degree of success" and credit Nunn-Lugar initiatives for no early post-Cold War loose nukes problems. In addition, they attribute part of these great successes to the extraordinary cooperation inside the Washington policy making community. Whether the ongoing efforts between the US, Russia and the United Nations can meet the high standards of the Nunn-Lugar programs remains to be seen. In retrospect, "denuclearizing" the Ukraine, Belorussia and Kazakhstan, has contributed to their region's stability and security. Bringing the same degree of effectiveness for similar outcomes is a worthy goal for US counter-proliferation efforts in Syria, as well as for the future security of the Middle East and the world.

The success of Nunn-Lugar weapons of mass destruction counter proliferation programs can be contrasted with the failure of the US approach in the Bill Clinton and George W. Bush Administrations in Iraq. These contrasts highlight the very real need for US national security reform, especially in the approach to MENA and the study of international, transnational, and US national and homeland security in the Mediterranean, geostrategic context. The 2003 US War in Iraq still gives us much to think about.

Richard Haass, an experienced State Department, Defense Department and National Security Council policy maker called it a war of "choice," as opposed to a war of "necessity."[24] According to Haass, Afghanistan was a necessary war, needed to defeat the regime that supported the 9/11 attacks on the United States. Iraq on the other hand was a war of choice, chosen for less than vital national interests to eliminate an evil dictator and his weapons of mass destruction programs, and redirect the Middle East towards democratic governance and capitalism. The Bush-43 Administration also highlighted ethical arguments, with the war justified as a moral obligation – for a great power to bring regime change to a hostile and bloody Iraq suffering under a dictator who had murdered, tortured and even gassed his own people.

The difficult decisions over war and peace are among the most well-researched by academics, especially historians, political scientists

DOI: 10.1057/9781137504081.0008

and international relations scholars. The national security team advising President Bush-43 included Cheney, Rumsfeld, Powell and Rice – who were all highly experienced in foreign and defense policy making and war. Rumsfeld and Cheney had served as White House chiefs of staff in the Ford Administration. Both were former Congress members. Rumsfeld was the youngest Secretary of Defense in US history under the honorable Gerald Ford, although only for one year. Dick Cheney was the Secretary of Defense during the 1990–1991 Gulf War. Colin Powell had been the National Security Advisor to President Reagan. He was also Chairman of the Joint Chiefs of Staff during the first Gulf War. The resume of the one professor in the President's inner circle, Dr. Condoleezza Rice, now at Stanford University, included real world experience on the Joint Chiefs of Staff and National Security Council. The efforts of the Bush-41 national security team on US-Russia relations during German reunification were truly transformational in world affairs. So the question remains: how did so many smart – and experienced – people get it so wrong? What accounts for these failures?

4.2.3   Is the US government not effective at long-term policy, strategy and planning?

Experienced practitioners have argued for years that there is no effective strategy office – one that aligns and integrates the US diplomatic, military and economic instruments of statecraft – within and across the US government. The once highly regarded State Department Policy Planning Staff has been relegated from the heights of the critical thinking done by containment architects George Kennan and Paul Nitze immediately after World War II to a speech writing and internal think tank. Containment is viewed with nostalgia by Cold War historians and security specialists. Historian John Lewis Gaddis points to Kennan's late 1940s approach to "containing" the Soviet threat as a "great" grand strategy, one that the US has not been able to replicate in the post-Cold War or post-911 periods. Gaddis points out the success in terms of the four decades of no wars with the Soviet Union, and no appeasement of the Soviet's expansionist aims.[25]

A recent policy review is the book of Richard, Haass, the current president of the Council on Foreign Relations, ran the State Department's policy shop for Secretary of State Colin Powell during the planning for the 2003 War. Haass's account in *War of Necessity, War of Choice*, includes a declassified, secret, "failed" policy paper on the problems expected

DOI: 10.1057/9781137504081.0008

in the reconstruction of Iraq. Haass laments his, as well as Secretary Powell, being out of the loop and ineffectual in contributing to the core Administration decision making process. So if not in the State Department where should major policies be debated and analyzed? In the National Security Council? Subject to presidential decision making styles and experiences, time constraints, and electoral pressures?

4.2.4   Does current Washington DC partisanship paralyze government decision-making?

To be sure, partisanship between Democrats and Republicans may be at an all-time high in DC – and the political bickering clearly does not stop at the water's edge. But has the Vietnam War when people reflect on the "bipartisanship" of the Cold War era been forgotten? What about the Church Committee review of the CIA in the 1970s? Among other things, the agency was accused of experiments in mind-control drugs, foreign assassinations and domestic spying. Consider Iran Contra during the Reagan Administration? Recall the episodes involving national security staffer, Oliver North, running covert operations out of the White House, to trade arms with Iran for freeing American hostages in Lebanon, as well as violating Congressional intent and US laws to fund Nicaraguan Contra forces. Note that of the 14 people charged criminally in Iran Contra, four received felony convictions after jury trials, and seven pleaded guilty to felonies or misdemeanors.

There are plenty of other examples of failed policy and decision making throughout the post-Cold War and other periods of American history as well. The post-Gulf War period that resulted in the Iraqi Shia and Kurds was left to the mercy of Saddam Hussein in 1991? During the Clinton presidency, in Somalia, a failed state, the well-intentioned Bush-41 Administration efforts at famine relief were followed by the Blackhawk Down chase for a rogue warlord. Rwanda, also during the Clinton Administration, included the tragic United Nations and US failures to prevent the slaughter of 500,000 to one million people. In sum, the US record in foreign affairs remains mixed in Democratic and Republican administrations. Political partnership or bipartisanship in Washington cannot account for policy successes or failures.

For another more recent update, former State Department Iran expert Vali Nasr's book, *Dispensable Nation*, explains the policymaking muddle among the White House, military, CIA and the State Department.

DOI: 10.1057/9781137504081.0008

Democratic political appointee Nasr bluntly criticizes the Obama Administration for ignoring the pragmatic approach of seasoned diplomat Richard Holbrooke.[26] The late Richard Holbrooke was chief architect of the Dayton Accords that ended the war in the former Yugoslavia and became Obama's special envoy for Afghanistan-Pakistan. Nasr pointedly criticizes the White House for seeking to pivot towards Asia and away from the very real threats and challenges of the Muslim world, and for placing electoral politics ahead of national security concerns.

4.2.5   Are national security affairs in an age of globalization just too complicated?

There is an argument that the issues of war and peace, in an age of globalization, with the threats of shadowy terrorists, with the deep seated sectarian and ethnic divisions make it too complicated to do much better. After all, the foreign policy elites and government officials mentioned above are all smart people. Many have spent their adult lives in foreign and defense agencies as well as in military service. Probably if there were answers they would know.

But time after time we find out that they really do not know. See the CIA's reports on the "intelligence" drawn from Curveball the Iraqi taxi driver in Germany, who is now described as habitual liar who was intent on personally bringing down the Iraqi regime. Curveball, we now know, identified as former Iraqi Chemical engineer, Rafid Amed Alan al-Janabi, invented the claims about Iraq weapons of mass destruction that became part of the narrative by Secretary Powell in his 2003 UN Security Council briefing, as well as the intelligence community's pre-2003 war National Intelligence Estimate on Iraq.

See also the decisions by Paul Bremer the head of the Iraq Coalition Provisional Authority, in ignoring his staff and disbanding the Iraq Army, firing Iraqi government officials (Baathists), and having to reverse course in short order after planning for a longer reign as America's proconsul.[27]

Or read the 9/11 Commission Report on systemic United States government failures before, during and after 9/11. Recent scorecards by a variety of experts, including the "Tenth Anniversary Report Card" by the 2001 Hamilton-Kean 911 Commission, continue to site the government's failing grades in meeting the recommended changes to policy, strategy and organizational reforms.

DOI: 10.1057/9781137504081.0008

4.2.6   Perhaps no one really knows how to fix these problems?

Iraq in 2003, unfortunately, is not the exception that proves the rule. It is a prime example of why some argue that major reforms are long overdue or, as most agree, that at the very least these problems are worthy of serious, presidential attention. The Project on National Security Reform, in two volumes of case studies of the post-World War II era, concludes that the national security system is antiquated and dangerous, and undermines the efforts of all those charged with protecting US national security. After two years of serious study, recommendations in the project's final 2011 report include the critical needs for improving: "comprehensive strategy; foresight and anticipatory governance; strategic management; interagency high-performance teaming; integrated and flexible national security resourcing; the role of Congress; public-private partnering and global networking; and our greatest strength – human capital."[28] On July 31, 2012 the Project on National Security Reform posted a press release that they were going out of business and pointing out that their efforts to transform the national security system had failed.

One dimension of the problem is that the US government's longstanding planning, programming and budgeting processes are designed for ordinary times and there is more internal, government red-tape than would ever be tolerated in the private sector. For instance, see the Special Inspector General of Iraq Reconstruction reports on the waste, fraud and abuse in the spending of the Coalition Provisional Authority in Iraq or in the corresponding program evaluations in Afghanistan.[29] In the rush to begin the necessary military operations in Afghanistan and the war of choice in Iraq, there was no time to get the accountants, contractors, auditors and lawyers on board.

Congressional oversight and its Constitutional responsibilities to provide critical and timely assessments of administration policy, strategy, and operations, all are cited in the need for national security policy reforms. In general, the cost of opposition to a popular war, in a time of national emergency, clearly requires a strong political will as well as expertise in foreign and defense affairs. It has been argued that overwhelming Congressional votes in support of 2003 executive branch initiatives (such as the use of force Iraq, the Patriot Act, etc.) in the immediate post-9/11 period reflects lessons learned from administration opponents in 1990 – those who opposed the Persian Gulf War and suffered the political consequences of Nay votes.

DOI: 10.1057/9781137504081.0008

The Bush-43 themes have now been turned into caricatures, screening out much of the real substance over the policy debates and lessons to be learned. So, the litany of wrong statements bears repeating. Vice President Dick Cheney warned of threatening Iraqi weapons of mass destruction and National Security Advisor Condoleezza Rice raised concerns about uncertainty over Iraq WMD programs leading to a future mushroom cloud. The Director of Central Intelligence called the case for Iraq weapons of mass destruction a slam dunk. At the United Nations, Secretary of State Colin Powell warned of secretive mobile biological weapons laboratories. Deputy of Defense Paul Wolfowitz (a former ambassador, Senate staffer, political science professor, and international affairs school dean) forecast US troops being met as liberators and greeted with flowers. He also projected using Iraq oil revenues to finance their own reconstruction. In retrospect, the list of policy and intelligence shortcomings is long.

In the end, however, it is still fair to ask why senior government officials did not know better than to think, or even say, that it would be relatively easy to overthrow a long-term dictator, reestablish a government, reconstruct a devastated country, create a civil society and depart in short order. It is also relevant and important to also ask why the national security systems, interagency processes, and ultimately the US government – institutions, organizations and people – all failed. Lessons can be learned, or the potential for real learning to develop a deeper understanding of the recurring problems, as well as the opportunities for pragmatic reforms to improve future effectiveness in approaching MENA geopolitics, will surely be lost.

4.2.7   Is there a shortage of effective leaders in international affairs?

One way to gain deeper insights into the leadership challenges facing the US is thinking about the role of individuals as leaders as well as the US governments' leadership roles domestically, regionally and internationally. Since letting President Obama know about his desire to retire as Secretary of Defense in 2011, Robert Gates made a number of significant speeches to core military groups – Army, Navy, Air Force and Marines – as well as the defense industry, leaving each with a blunt assessment his views on their current state of affairs, as well as some tasks to think about for the future of their service and the long-term security of the US. In his memoirs, *Duty,* he offers his long-term experience in highlighting problems as well as approaches for improving

DOI: 10.1057/9781137504081.0008

US policymaking and international relations. Recent research on effective senior leadership provides important ideas in recognizing the elements for success. To sum up a large literature, Robert Gates can be characterized as a "smart" leader, a "good" boss and a "noble" public servant.[30]

4.2.8 The smart international leader

Harvard University professor and former Harvard Kennedy School Dean, Joseph Nye has popularized the notion of smart power.[31] That idea is to blend the soft power skills of emotional intelligence, communications and vision, with the hard power skills of building organizations and coalitions, along with broad political skills (he calls this contextual intelligence) to understand evolving environments, capitalizing on trends, and adjusting one's leadership style to followers needs. At a 2003 Pentagon press briefing, when asked about whether he was considering using more "soft power" in the US approach in Iraq, Rumsfeld brusquely responded: "I don't know what it means."[32]

Gates, on the other hand, followed Secretary of State Hillary Clinton's adoption of smart power as part of her emphasis on 21st Century Statecraft. The new 3 D's of Diplomacy-Development-Defense interagency cooperation between Gates and Secretary of State's Condoleezza Rice, and then between Gates and Hillary Clinton marked an abrupt turnaround. Memoirs by Bush-43 officials are all consistent in pointing out the frosty relationship and open warfare between Rumsfeld and both Colin Powell and Condoleezza Rice. While far from perfect, the Gates-Clinton public partnership contributed to the more positive relationship among the State Department, the Agency for International Development, and the Defense Department, as well as a more balanced consideration of blending diplomacy, economics and military force in American national security policy. While the bureaucratic turf battles between the Pentagon and Foggy Bottom have continued, as usual, in the struggles for resources and missions, there has been a marked ascendance of the idea of smart power and this in large measure should be credited to Gates' adaptive leadership style and coalition building skills – those that Nye would prescribe as essential to good leadership.

4.2.9 The statesman as a good leader

Leadership researchers have referred to the idea of "toxic" leadership, or those who rely solely on commanding and pacesetting styles, as opposed

DOI: 10.1057/9781137504081.0008

to more nuanced visionary, coaching, democratic and affiliative styles. No doubt, Rumsfeld would be characterized as commanding and pace-setting and, most likely, would see that as a compliment. Emotional intelligence (EI) experts, like Daniel Goleman, Richard Boyatzis and Annie McKee tell us that the research is clear – over the long haul, toxic leaders are bad for your and their own health and are likely to contribute to organizational disasters.[33] EI and executive development coaches, like Stanford's Robert Sutton, will tell you to develop a golf bag filled with a variety of styles that are appropriate for different contexts.

The contrast of the perceived single-minded Rumsfeld and the multi-dimensional Gates again is interesting in terms of gauging the relative effectiveness of senior executives. For instance, the late-term Bush-43 Iraq surge, during Gates' early tenure as Secretary of Defense, is seen as saving the US effort in Iraq. In contrast, the Rumsfeld 2003 post-war "stabilization" period has been critically reviewed as a "fiasco."[34]

In terms of accountability, Gates is known to have fired or replaced more senior military officers and defense officials than did Rumsfeld. Recent articles critical of Gates, by national security experts such as Lawrence Korb and Paul Pillar, point out several senior officials that Gate replaced. Examples include the removal of the Middle East regional commander and Afghanistan field commander over troop-level policy disputes. The Army's senior civilian official and surgeon general were removed after the *Washington Post* wrote a series of articles about the inadequate support for wounded soldiers at Walter Reed. The Secretary of the Air Force and the Air Force Chief of Staff were also removed after a series of incidents, including mistaken loading of nuclear warheads in 2007 from North Dakota to Louisiana. Gates also raised concerns about the slow response of the Air Force to increasing the production and deployment of drones for the counterinsurgency campaigns in Iraq and Afghanistan. No doubt these actions, difficult in peacetime or wartime, will be open to debate in case studies of senior leader "accountability" for years to come in public affairs programs as well as business schools. Nevertheless, as Gates said in quoting Theodore Roosevelt at a recent commencement speech: "The average ... cannot be kept high unless the standard of the leaders is very much higher." To hold those high standards, in full knowledge of the exposure to personal attacks, Gates goes on to point out that leaders at times have to have the courage "to chart a new course," "to do what is right," and to "stand alone." Speaking truth to power is difficult, and so is speaking truth to organizations that are not performing up to their capabilities.

DOI: 10.1057/9781137504081.0008

The need to speak bluntly about the strengths and weaknesses of leadership and organizations is one area where we think that Gates and Rumsfeld would agree. Nevertheless, Donald Rumsfeld, despite his many tough decisions, such as restructuring the Cold War military, if not wholly "transforming" the Defense Department as he intended to do, and responding to the rapid changes of the post 9/11 world, will continue to be criticized by many inside and outside the DC beltway as a toxic leader and a bad boss. For instance, Condoleezza Rice recently broke her silence on the Rumsfeld criticism of her performance as Bush-43's national security advisor, by characterizing Don Rumsfeld as just plain old "grumpy."[35]

Yet, despite both secretaries continual battling with the Pentagon bureaucracy and the Congress in calling for major reforms to enhance the Defense Department's effectiveness, in comparison to Donald Rumsfeld, Robert Gates will be known as the good boss. In essence, the sometimes overly dramatic press coverage of the wrestler Rumsfeld and the Eagle Scout Gates oversimplify the reality of life at the highest levels of government.

Gates' glowing *60 Minutes* profile, in pointing out his reputation as the "Soldiers' Secretary,"[36] adds to the good boss commentary. No doubt, future defense secretaries will be encouraged, probably repeatedly, to think: What would Bob Gates do? Personal leadership characteristics are of course important as well as the senior officials' roles in guiding their institutions.

4.2.10 The noble public servant: grounded, pragmatic, and realistic; and romantic, idealistic and optimistic

Gates is also widely recognized for publically promoting the ideal of the nobility of public service. George H.W. Bush is noted for saying that "public service is a noble calling." And good leadership, leadership that Nye points out must be both effective and ethical, requires "dogged effort" and also calls for leaders of character. Furthermore, the unique naming of the school was to be a school of "government and public service."[37] Interim Dean, Robert Gates was engaged directly in the Bush School's emphasis on designing an academic program devoted to educating principled leaders for careers of public service. These thoughts are reflected in Gates' own words in his 2007 speech, upon returning to Texas A&M University, after once again being called by a president to serve his country as Secretary of Defense: "In our heart of hearts, [public servants] are romantics, idealists and optimists. We actually believe we can make a difference, make the lives of others better."[38]

People who report on those who have worked with Gates will tell that he is grounded, pragmatic and realistic rather than romantic, idealistic and optimistic. His essential realistic and pragmatic nature comes through repeatedly in his autobiography, *From the Shadows*, about his CIA career. Even then he clearly recognized the political nature of national security policymaking in terms of a public servant's working cooperatively with the executive and legislative branches of government while ultimately serving the nations interests. In short, his reflections hold a reverence for American political institutions and its public servants at all levels of government. In a sober assessment of the highs and lows of public service, Gates writes:

> The White House is a poignant place. .... And it seems to me that those who live and work there, if they are completely honest with themselves, with rare exception the most the most vivid memories are not of victory and joy but of crisis and defeat – and, for the fortunate few, of one or two occasions of historical importance. This is why character counts for so much in a President. In the White House, the elation of victory is fleeting and the burden of responsibility is enduring.[39]

4.2.11   Redemption: fixing leadership, institutions, and policymaking

In sum, the smart leader knows how to use "common sense" to adapt to the reality of his/her environment, and at the same time to inspire followers, and future leaders, to press forward and to be prepared get back up after hard knocks – and continually face the burden of responsibility. The record of Robert Gates as a smart leader, good boss and public servant will be assessed and argued by a variety of historians and pundits has begun and will continue for years to come. For future generations, for those who will have to continue to work to improve US-EU-MENA relations, it is likely that in Robert Gates we have an example of one of the most influential leaders of this generation – a senior leader who will continue to stress that there are both burdensome responsibilities and true nobility in the meaningful work of international public servants.

There is of course much more work to be done to address the pressing issues following the early post-Arab Spring period. Research that helps

DOI: 10.1057/9781137504081.0008

understand the narratives of the post-World War II evolution of the EU, NATO and the US national security establishments – institutions, organizations and policymaking processes – and current EU and NATO national security and homeland security issues are all important. A focus on current events without a deeper understanding of the founding and evolution of policies and agencies will hamper any attempts to build a shared perception of developing ways to go forward.[40]

As discussed earlier, it will be important to examine the roles of the key players, both leaders and agencies, engaged in the US, EU and NATO, and MENA international security policy, strategy and decision-making. Understanding cultural differences in terms of leadership and leader development in intercultural setting should receive additional attention in the study of geopolitics. Gaining intercultural perspectives will also require designing comparative research projects to study the academic literature, government policy documents, and think tank analyses across MENA and Western governments. The role of international affairs experts then should include developing individual subject matter expertise in contemporary national security policy issues, multilateral organizations and international institutions.

Especially in the American side of the Atlantic, there remains a significant gap in preparing emerging leaders for their roles in international affairs as well as contemporary transatlantic and Mediterranean security issues.[41] For instance, the Partnership for 21st Century calls for reinforcing skills in six areas;

1 The traditional core academic subjects.
2 Twenty-first century content, including global, financial and environmental awareness.
3 Learning and thinking skills, including creativity, critical thinking, problem solving, communication and collaboration.
4 Information and communications technology skills.
5 Life and career skills, including time management, group work and leadership.
6 Twenty-first century assessments that accurately measure the other five skills.[42]

For an aspiring international leader, learning these skills in the cultural contexts of the Middle East and North Africa will require a lifetime of effort. There is no shortage of experts who will urge caution and strategic patience when addressing the current MENA threats as well as the

DOI: 10.1057/9781137504081.0008

extensive efforts that will be required to build on the aspirations of the public involved in the post-Arab Spring nations. Gauging the magnitude of the problems facing the United States and EU in their roles for advancing local political, economic and social development will remain the work of the generation of current and emerging leaders. Identifying the nature of the threats and the priorities for defense, diplomacy and development policy is an important first step. This will also require important reflections on the part of US and other Western leaders about fixing their own internal agencies, processes and approaches. Current as well as future leaders should be encouraged to learn more from current and past efforts and consider new ways to address the threats and opportunities of national, regional and human security in building stronger relationships among the US and EU and the countries and people of the Middle East and North Africa.

Notes

1   Rosa Balfour, "The Arab Spring, the changing Mediterranean, and the EU: tools as a substitute for strategy?" *European Policy Centre Policy Brief* (June 2011); Richard Youngs, "The EU and the Arab Spring: from munificence to geo-strategy," *FRIDE Policy Brief* no. 100 (October 2011).

2   Oded Eran, "The West Responds to the Arab Spring," *Strategic Assessment* 14, no. 2 (July 2011), p. 15; Uri Dadush and Michele Dunne, "American and European Responses to the Arab Spring: What's the Big Idea?" The *Washington Quarterly* 34, no. 4 (Fall 2011), p. 132.

3   Massimo D'Alema, "The Arab Spring and Europe's Chance," *Project Syndicate*, October 25, 2011.

4   Dadush and Dunne, "American and European Responses to the Arab Spring," p. 136.

5   Eran, "The West Responds to the Arab Spring," p. 25.

6   D'Alema, "The Arab Spring and Europe's Chance."

7   Balfour, "The Arab Spring."

8   Sergio Fabbrini and Amr Yossef, "Obama's wavering: US foreign policy on the Egyptian crisis, 2011–13," *Contemporary Arab Affairs* 8, no. 1 (2015): 69.

9   Yousry Mustapha, "Donors' Responses to Arab Uprisings: Old Medicine in New Bottles?" *IDS Bulletin* 43, no. 1 (January 2012): 101–106.

10   Daron Acemoglu and James Robinson, *Why Nations Fail: The Origins of Power, Prosperity, and Poverty* (New York: Crown Business, 2012).

11   Kaplan, *Fixing Fragile States*, pp. 53–54.

12   Migdal, *Strong Societies and Weak States*, pp. 269–271.

DOI: 10.1057/9781137504081.0008

13 *Ibid.*, pp. 274–275.

14 *Ibid.*, p. 275.

15 *The Economist*, "Lee Kuan Yew: The wise man of the East," March 22, 2015, http://www.economist.com/news/asia/21646869-lee-kuan-yew-made-singapore-paragon-development-authoritarians-draw-wrong-lessons-his.

16 Omar Ashour, "Finishing the Job: Security Sector Reform After the Arab Spring," *World Politics Review*, May 28, 2013, http://www.brookings.edu/research/articles/2013/05/28-security-sector-reform-mena-ashour.

17 See Alan J. Kuperman, "Obama's Libya Debacle: How a Well-Meaning Intervention Ended in Failure," Foreign Affairs 94, no. 2 (March/April 2015): 66–77.

18 Mohamed el-Khatib, "Al-Sisi: Our Aim is to Preserve the State," Egypt News, Dec. 12, 2014, http://www.egynews.net/السيسي-عابداللـل-واوملفكركن-هدفنال-ا/.

19 Jreisat, *Politics Without Process*, p. 89.

20 Jerisat, "The Arab World: Reform or Stalemate," p. 433.

21 This is an excerpt from Joseph R. Cerami, *Leadership and Policy Innovation – From Clinton To Bush: Countering the Proliferation of Weapons of Mass Destruction* (London: Routledge, 2013).

22 George Bush and Brent Scowcroft, *A World Transformed* (New York: Alfred A. Knopf, 1998).

23 Ashton B. Carter and William J. Perry, *Preventive Defense: A New Security Strategy for America* (Washington, D.C.: Brookings Institution Press, 1999).

24 Richard N. Haass, *War of Necessity, War of Choice: A Memoir of Two Iraq Wars* (New York: Simon & Schuster, 2009).

25 John Lewis Gaddis, *Strategies of Containment: A Critical Appraisal of American National Security Policy during the Cold War* (New York: Oxford University Press, 2005).

26 Vali Nasr, *The Dispensable Nation: American Foreign Policy in Retreat* (New York: Doubleday, 2013).

27 "Colin Powell regrets Iraq war intelligence: 'Former US secretary of state says information he provided leading to the invasion of Iraq is a "blot" on his record,' Aljazeera, 11 Sep 2001, http://www.aljazeera.com/news/americas/2011/09/20119116916873488.html.

28 That document, and others including a comprehensive study for building an integrated national security professional system, is at http://www.pnsr.org/.

29 See the reports of the SIGAR at http://www.sigar.mil/.

30 Robert M. Gates, *Duty: Memoirs of a Secretary at War* (New York: Alfred A. Knopf, 2014).

31 Joseph S. Nye Jr., *The Powers to Lead* (New York: Oxford University Press, 2008). One book highlighting diverse views on the US leadership role in the current international environment is Melvyn P. Leffler and Jeffrey W. Legro,

DOI: 10.1057/9781137504081.0008

eds., *To Lead the World: American Strategy after the Bush Doctrine* (New York: Oxford University Press, 2008).

32   Joseph S. Nye Jr., "Think Again: Soft Power," *ForeignPolicy.com*, February 23, 2006, http://foreignpolicy.com/2006/02/23/think-again-soft-power/.

33   Daniel Goleman, Richard Boyatzis, and Annie McKee, *Primal Leadership: Realizing the Power of Emotional Intelligence* (Boston: Harvard Business School Press, 2002).

34   Thomas E. Ricks, 2006, *Fiasco: The American Military Adventure in Iraq*, New York: The Penguin Press.

35   Jennifer Epstein, "condoleezza Rice on Donald Rumsfeld: Wrong, 'grumpy'", *POLITICO*, April 28, 2011, http://www.politico.com/news/stories/0411/53814.html.

36   Katie Couric, CBS News 60 Minutes, "Robert Gates: The soldiers' secretary," May 15, 2011, http://www.cbsnews.com/videos/robert-gates-the-soldiers-secretary/.

37   The Bush School of Texas A&M University was established by the 41st President in 1997. The graduate school offers master's degrees in public service and administration and in international affairs. See: http://bush.tamu.edu/.

38   Robert Gates: Our founding fathers' belief in public service is due a revival," *The Independent*, December 22, 2009, http://www.independent.co.uk/voices/commentators/robert-gates-our-founding-fathers-belief-in-public-service-is-due-a-revival-1847245.html.

39   Robert M. Gates, *From the Shadows: The Ultimate Insider's Story of Five Presidents and How They Won the Cold War* (New York: Simon & Schuster, 1996), p. 574.

40   For examples of this kind of agency and institutional research see: Amy B. Zegart, *Flawed by Design: The Evolution of the CIA, JCS, and NSC* (Stanford: Stanford University Press, 1999); Douglas T. Stuart, *Creating the National Security State: A History of the Law That Transformed America* (Princeton: Princeton University Press, 2008); Aaron L. Friedberg, *In the Shadow of the Garrison State: America's Anti-Statism and Its Cold War Grand Strategy* (Princeton: Princeton University Press, 2000); and James R. Locher III, *Victory on the Potomac: The Goldwater-Nichols Unifies the Pentagon* (College Station: Texas A&M University Press, 2002).

41   Joel I. Klein, and Condoleezza Rice, and Julia Levy, *U.S. Education Reform and National Security,* Independent Task Force Report No. 68 (New York: Council on Foreign Relations, 2012).

42   "Framework for 21st Century Learning," Partnership for 21st Century Skills, http://www.p21.org/.

DOI: 10.1057/9781137504081.0008

Conclusion

Abstract: *Redemption from the "original sin," that is Arab state weakness/failure, requires first a recognition of the problem. Old approaches by the EU and the United States have not worked and therefore should only be incorporated within the overall approach of state-building. State-building would basically involve re-building bureaucracies in order to have a state that is enforcing law, providing services appropriately, and managing the state resources by an efficient bureaucracy, which is the redemption we propose for the Arab world. The role of the US cannot be overlooked even if it appears as though it is withdrawing from the Middle East to more pressing strategic interests in the Far East. We proposed restoring America's leadership to help re-building the Arab state. This restoration, in turn, requires a reform in the US decision-making to prevent a repetition of the mistakes of the last several years of American mismanagement of the region.*

Yossef, Amr and Joseph R. Cerami. *The Arab Spring and the Geopolitics of the Middle East: Emerging Security Threats and Revolutionary Change.* Basingstoke: Palgrave Macmillan, 2015. DOI: 10.1057/9781137504081.0009.

This book has been critical of the way the "authority vacuum" that followed the revolutions against authoritarian regimes in Tunisia, Egypt, Libya and Syria – affecting the state's ability to deliver basic public services which influenced citizens' human security and state's national security – has been treated and understood by the established conventional wisdom with its emphasis on the absence of legitimacy (in the form of national coherence and democratic governance) as the cause of instability.

We have suggested instead that conventional wisdom is both conceptually limited and empirically deficient, and that the failure in "state capacity" that has caused the rise of religious, tribal and ethnic divisions, because it was these affiliations that could compensate the citizens of the absence of the state. It was the deterioration of government services, as the polls in the four Arab countries (Egypt, Libya, Syria and Tunisia) indicate, that pushed the Arab populations to revolution in 2011. Unlike the democracy variable, which does not appear to be significantly different in these four countries, the "stateness" variable we propose – state strength in enforcing law and administering the public business efficiently though its bureaucracy – accounts for the variation in these countries different paths after four years of the uprising, which is quite consistent with the variation in the governance indicators.

The cases of Tunisia and Libya are comparatively telling. Post-independence, both were governed by authoritarian regimes, though their level of "stateness" varied significantly, where Tunisia exhibited attributes of a relatively stronger state than that of Libya. Consequently, the two countries also varied significantly in the paths events took taken in each of which following the fall of their respective authoritarian regimes. In itself, the weakness of "stateness" in these four Arab countries has been the result of historical processes, particularly throughout the 19th and 20th centuries, that inhibited the establishment and sustainment of strong state institutions.

Critical Security Studies, whose scholars have been pioneers in warning against the security threats that state weakness/failure presents have equally been insufficient in analyzing the Arab Spring thus far in that it has focused more on the occurrences in pre- and during the revolution time and less on those that have been taking place in the post-revolution time, or prescribing external solution to essentially internal problems.

Reviewing the double fall of the regimes and public order in Egypt, Syria, Tunisia and Libya, we have shown that the key role the security services played in not only maintaining authoritarian regimes but also

DOI: 10.1057/9781137504081.0009

keeping the state itself operating, explain a great deal of the turmoil in these Arab Spring countries. The fall of these security services, which constitutes in and of itself a symptom of the state weakness/failure, led to the enormous inward-directed and outward-directed security threats in these four countries. A clear example combining both is how the insecurity from violence and insecurity from want have contributed to the massive exodus of illegal immigrants from the MENA countries to the European Union across the Mediterranean.

We conclude by establishing that redemption from the "original sin" requires first and foremost a recognition of the problem, the state weakness/ failure in the Arab world in which the old approaches by the EU and the United States, ranging from providing economic and development aid to pushing premature democratic promotion, have not worked and therefore should only be incorporated within the overall approach of state-building. State-building, as we proposed above, far exceeds the traditional reform methods of providing training and consultancy, to basically re-building state bureaucracies in the four Arab Spring countries under study here. Enforcing law, providing services appropriately, and managing the state resources by an efficient bureaucracy is the redemption we seek for the Arab world, that has undergone revolutions that provide the ground for a new order of things in these countries. Nevertheless, the role of the indispensable nation, the United States, cannot be overlooked even if it appears in the Arab world as though it is withdrawing from the Middle East to more pressing strategic interests in the Far East. We proposed restoring America's leadership to help re-building the Arab state. This restoration, however, would not be in itself possible until the leadership and decision-making in the United States is reformed to guarantee that the future would not include a repetition of the mistakes of the last several years of American mismanagement of the region.

DOI: 10.1057/9781137504081.0009

Index

DOI: 10.1057/9781137504081.0010

DOI: 10.1057/9781137504081.0010

CPSIA information can be obtained
at www.ICGtesting.com
Printed in the USA
LVOW08*2345010617
536675LV00020B/731/P